7 Dumb Things We All Say

Smart Ways to Improve *EVERY* Relationship

Greg Alcorn

Printed in the United States of America.

ISBN-10: 1-947480-32-4
ISBN-13: 978-1-947480-32-2
Library of Congress Control Number: 2018962277

Designed by Joni McPherson, mcphersongraphics.com

INDIE BOOKS INTERNATIONAL, LLC
2424 VISTA WAY, SUITE 316
OCEANSIDE, CA 92054

www.indiebooksintl.com

Contents

Preface

This is not a page-turner, a book so exciting you can't put it down until you read it all. This is a book meant to be savored. Jump in anywhere. Come back to it and read a favorite section again. Keep it on your bookshelf and read it again and again. We all say dumb things (if you don't believe me, just ask my wife, Missie). The trick is not to say them repeatedly.

Greg Alcorn, Salisbury, North Carolina
September 2018

PART I

Why What You Say Matters

" My son is a corporate communications director.
He never calls and he never writes."

1

How Not to Lose Friends and Repel People

Dale Carnegie never ran a call center.

The world owes a debt to Carnegie, author of the classic book, *How to Win Friends and Influence People.*

When it comes to influence, I have picked up a thing or two in the last three decades. I have run customer service call centers for thirty years and I have listened in on twenty-one million calls. In that time, I have made and I have heard countless conversation blunders. That's right: the dumb things we all say.

The advice in this book is based on our proprietary research into what works and what does not work in conversations. Countless customer satisfaction surveys have given us the data to know how to win through better conversations in the twenty-first century.

Winning through better conversations was a theme of *How to Win Friends and Influence People*, a self-help book published in 1936. Over thirty million copies have been sold worldwide, making it one of the best-selling books of all time.

Carnegie's book contains colorful anecdotes, insightful wisdom, instruction in handling people, "winning" friends, bringing people around to your way of thinking, being a great leader, and successfully navigating home life. Carnegie's writing combines age-old truisms with the then-emerging field of psychology to present a handbook in human relations which was interesting and accessible.

The book that you are holding is applied psychology updated for our age. This is a subject I have studied to improve the quality of conversations which our customer advocates have with callers. My view is applied psychology is not manipulation; it is simply polite and respectful communication.

In other words, not saying dumb things when we communicate.

Sadly, communication skills are not taught in our schools as they should be. (If you ask me, the greatest time to teach communications skills would be the eighth grade, just before those awkward high school years. Trust me, I know the importance of learning the hard skills in schools, like reading, writing, and arithmetic. But those high school years and beyond would be a lot less awkward if teenagers had in their tool chests a few more communications soft skills.)

Once upon a time, soft skills mattered. Really mattered. Soft skills include the ability to have a great conversation. Having a conversation is like a friendly tennis match of serve and volley; of speaking and listening.

In my view, quality conversations today are rare. Sometimes these conversations are only used as a last resort when text sarcasm is missed, the wrong person was copied on an email, or a wrong attachment was attached. During those difficult times, a person needs all the conversation skills they can muster.

But what about *avoiding* difficult times? The purpose of this book is to provide soft skill conversation suggestions for those occasions when a powerful voice is needed and a laser-focused ear is wanted. I hope to open eyes to the joy and satisfaction of great dialogue and make it less rare.

No one expects anybody to read this book and become a conversation master. But if people read and seek to apply these communications skills, then they can expect to improve their proficiency.

Commands and Suggestions

In one memorable broadcast, Garrison Keillor, the former host of NPR's *Prairie Home Companion*, was comparing Episcopalians to other denominations. He said, "They're so liberal they have six commandments and four suggestions."

In my world of running call centers, it's mostly rules and commands. Fewer suggestions.

Yet, customer experience has some openings for suggestions. At our call centers, we combine the necessary disclosures and disclaimers with friendly, bonding, supportive words to provide the facts while promoting a good feeling. Many of our coaching fundamentals focus on voice inflection and the use of stimulating words and phrases. We often replace the simplest of responses with those that perk up the customer and make their day. Our associates have the freedom to suggest pleasantries.

For example, when a customer asks us, "How are you?" we might replace "fine," "good," or "well" with "terrific," "fantastic," or "excellent." Don't you like talking to people who feel fantastic? We strive to combine compliance with friendly service, and the results have been amazing.

Most of our work has an audio component to it, so we spend most of our education time on presentation skills and the rest of the time on compliance. It's a great combination of rules and suggestions.

PRINCIPLE

Focus on removing all the distractions around your presentations so the listener can concentrate easily on what is being said. If you know speaking quickly can be a distraction, then you can concentrate on slowing your pace.

Everyone can benefit from feedback on pace. People used to say I talked too fast, a rare accusation for a Southerner like myself. When I listened to recordings, I realized I was, in fact, too rapid in my speech. Now I'm more conscious of my speech pace today, and I hope my slowing down helps listeners feel more comfortable when I'm speaking. Still, every time I listen to my recorded voice, I always say: "Do I sound like that?"

Smartphone apps make it so easy to do many things, including recording your own voice. Try recording a conversation sometime. Listen to what you sound like. Once you get over the "Do I sound like that?" aspect, really listen to what you sound like. Then make a choice to change.

Why Communication Skills Really Matter

By picking the right words, at the right time, and saying them in the right way, anyone can avoid uncomfortable conversations. These conversations can help lead us to get what we want in life. And when done right, conversations make others happy to help us get what we want.

In the business world, everyone wants high customer satisfaction. By following the advice in this book, I guarantee you can create higher customer satisfaction scores.

What I liked about Carnegie's book is it is an action-oriented book to improve satisfaction in life. His goal in writing was to equip readers to better handle life's situations. While humans have not changed that much in eighty years, the demands of modern life have accelerated.

To quote Carnegie, "This introduction, like most introductions, is already too long." So, let's begin by examining the seven blunders. Please turn immediately to the next chapter to begin.

But first, consider these examples of what to say and what not to say. Each chapter will include these practical applications.

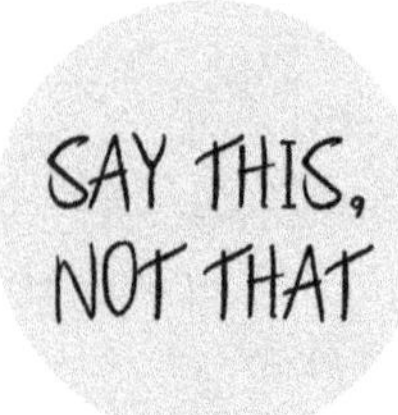

How Not to Lose Friends and Repel People

SAY THIS	NOT THAT
I am great	I am OK
I know exactly what you mean	Yeah, whatever
I'm so sorry that happened	Sorry, that's how it goes
Tell me your story	Where are you from?
Listen to this	Here's a funny story
That's fine	You're fine
We're open until five	We close at five

What to Say and How to Say It: Fixing Seven Common Blunders

This book asks you to make a *paradigm shift* in your communications. We all have assumptions about how the world works. A paradigm shift is when an important change happens, when the usual way of thinking or doing something is replaced by a new and different way.

Let me illustrate with a story I call "The Power of the Orange Cone."

Do you believe that orange traffic cones have some mystical power?

You have seen countless conical markers used on roads and highways, usually denoting that repairs are being done or an area is off limits. You can have 5,000 parking spaces, 6,000 cars, and one orange cone; no one will park in the space with the cone. That space is off limits. Only the cone master knows who gets to park there.

What are the "orange cones" in communication? Subjects that are off-limits. These include polarizing issues, medical conditions, and previous arguments we do not want to discuss again.

When I was board chair of Salisbury Academy, we started meetings with a story and a prayer. One month, the orange cone was the story.

About a decade previously, I had witnessed a car swipe an orange cone protecting some street maintenance. The cone flipped, careened like a bowling pin, and was hit by a following minivan. I was driving behind the minivan. The cone lodged under my car for about 100 yards before spitting out the rear and into the middle of the road.

I stopped, put the orange cone on the sidewalk, and drove away. Then, the ten-year new life of the cone started. The cone guarded the sidewalk for a year. Nobody touched it. Then the cone moved to the grass beside the curb. The homeowner mowed around it. *Then*, the cone moved across the road, becoming a sentry for a water meter. For the next eight years, the cone did not move. The cone did lose its shine, but it did not move.

What's the point? Paradigm acceptance. Everyone *assumed* the cone had a higher purpose. That is The Power of the Orange Cone. Yet, I knew the back story and enjoyed watching the cone hold power for a decade. (Undeserved power, I might add.)

The moral of the story: Don't assume what you are doing is the best way.

At my company, we use that orange cone story to look at our processes, our language, and our relationships. Are they as valuable today as they were yesterday? What is the source of the words? Are they the best terms? Are we protecting yesterday or promoting tomorrow?

I wish you great success with your upcoming communications paradigm shift.

PRINCIPLE

Check for orange cones in your life. What habits are not serving you? What are the off-limits topics? Be brave. Ask friends what they like about you and what your areas of improvement are (that's code for what bugs them about you). Prepare to have your feelings hurt and having even better friends.

The Seven Common Blunders

To improve every relationship, there are four magic words in the English language: "Say this, not that."

The first step in fixing common communication blunders is to know what those blunders are so you can say something the smart way and not the dumb way.

Nobody wants to say dumb things. But we all do. The first step towards reducing the number of dumb things you say is to know what the dumb things are. Based on thirty years of research with millions and millions of conversations, here are my top seven blunders, in rank order.

1. **Using Bad Bookends.** The first and biggest blunder is starting and ending what you say with the wrong phrasing. Conversation bookends are the small

comments or questions just before or right after a full statement or request for action. Be better with your starting and ending bookends. OK?

2. **Starting with Wrong First Words.** The second biggest blunder is starting off wrong with the first few words. Are you familiar with the adage, "Getting off on the wrong foot"? Conversations have first impressions, and they begin with your first three words. Hint: one of the words should be the other person's name.

3. **Not Choosing Your Words Well.** The third biggest blunder is choosing negative words over positive words. The words you choose paint a picture for the listener. Your words express your attitude and your personality. Keep it positive. Don't start a sentence with the word "no."

4. **Poor Questions and Bad Listening.** The fourth biggest blunder is the poor use of mouth and ears. Meaningful questions always stay on subject, keep a conversation moving forward, and ensure the other person feels heard and understood. Becoming a better listener is easier than you might think. It starts by committing to be a great listener and making an active choice to listen. Ask good questions and *really* listen. This is the "You have two ears and one mouth" principle.

5. **Focus-on-Me Attitude.** The fifth biggest blunder is to have a *me, me, me* attitude. Making it all about you is a turn off for them. Take the *I* and *me* statements out of your conversations and put

in the word you. This is not a technique, this is an attitude. *What do you think about me?*

6. **Wrong Tone.** The sixth biggest blunder is not saying your words with the proper tone of voice. People feel more comfortable with pleasant, variable tone quality. Voice tone is made up of rate, pitch, and volume. Think tone and don't drone. Don't talk like a Valley Girl or a mountain man (more about that in a later chapter).

7. **Not Diffusing Difficult Drama.** The seventh biggest blunder is creating drama or letting drama escalate. Stressful conversations, or drama, can be avoided by mastering word selection, listening, and questioning skills. Drama can be inevitable, however. Most stressful situations can be defused when you apply the three *R*s: recognize, restate, and reassure. Ask others: "What would *you* like to see happen?"

Checklist to Improve Every Relationship

This book is to help you at work and at home. First, let me ask you four questions:

1. Do you walk into a room and say: "Here I am"? Or do you say: "There you are"?

2. Do you speak with someone or at someone?

3. Do you have a conversational volley or just two parallel monologues?

4. Do you listen or just wait to talk again?

All of us have a communications persona. A *persona* is the aspect of your personality that is perceived by others. Put another way, this is how others perceive you based on what you are putting out to the world

Consider those perceptions for a moment. As the ancient philosophers advised, first know thyself. The following are questions anyone can ask when evaluating their own communication skills.

Here is a checklist of points to ask when gauging your communication persona:

- ✔ **Talk time.** If you talk all the time, you only learn what you already know. In a great conversation, the talk time for each person is 50 percent.
- ✔ **Stay on point.** It's frustrating to be in a conversation that jumps from one subject to the next without completion. Usually, dueling monologues are occurring. Try to stay on the other person's subject until they have told you everything that is important to them.
- ✔ **Segue.** Most of us can't spell this word, much less define it or practice it regularly. A *segue* (pronounced "seg-way") is simply a bridge. Learn to connect subjects by bridging them together: *"Your vacation reminds me of Disneyworld; have you ever been there? I have."*
- ✔ **Be Sincere.** Do you know someone whose voice changes depending on whom they talk to? You can tell when someone is genuine because they treat everyone the same.

- ✔ **Listen.** I think it's easier and more rewarding to ask questions and listen than to talk and talk and talk. The best way to be a great listener is to ask lots of good questions.
- ✔ **Good questions.** Good questions are open-ended and nonjudgmental. You know you've asked a good question when the response comes in the form of lots of sentences. Bad questions make you feel like you are being interrogated. Bad questions usually elicit one-word answers.
- ✔ **Thank you.** The two words everyone wants to hear. A good persona usually prompts a lot of "thank you" statements. Hope you have a great conversation today. Thank you.

Principles to Improve Relationships

Hall of Fame football coaching great Lou Holtz set 107 goals when he was young. As of this writing, he has achieved 102.

Holtz was an assistant coach at a small school when he wrote his goals and went on to become head coach at Notre Dame, which was one of his goals. He also set goals to skydive, read the Bible cover to cover, and be enshrined in the College Football Hall of Fame, which happened in 2008.

Personally, I strive to lead a principle-driven life. I have principles in leadership, teamwork, learning, communication, and almost every area of business and life. I have a goal of establishing 100 major principles for success. Here are some of my principles, inspired by Holtz, around selling yourself.

- **First Things First.** When you meet someone for the first time, start with a firm handshake, solid eye contact, and say the person's name. I've used several time management tools over the year. The best advice I got early on was from William Virtue. This gentle giant of a man was the owner's father at the metals company where I began my career. He was a longtime outside sales guy in the metals industry. He looked over my shoulder one day as I was making my to-do list and said, "Find the one thing on the list that you *don't want* to do and *do it first*. That way, the dread and anxiousness won't weigh down and slow down all the other activities."

- **Monopolize the Listening.** Be a world-class listener by first being a world-class questioner. Interesting people are those who are interested in you. That damn Ed Norvell. He's a successful attorney and community leader. We run in the same circles. Every time I'd see him at a party or the gym, he would ask me questions. Good questions. Thought-provoking questions. "I like him," I'd think. "Heck, I hardly know him, but he knows a lot about me. He is interested in me." Now, I tried to copy that principle of asking great questions, like Ed does. Interesting people are those interested in you.

- **Dress for Success.** Dress to the level you want to be promoted to. Business dress is different from social dress. In business, it's always, I mean *always*, better to slightly overdress. I appreciate when a person is well-dressed and well-prepared from the beginning. Make sure your clothes match (I need help from my wife on this one). Err on the side of a conservative look. Make sure your shoes are shined. Prepare for the unexpected. Have your car cleaned and the front seat open. I had to take a client to the *hospital* one time to be with his wife. I carry a small Swiss Army knife and a handkerchief. Where I am from, a *man* carries a knife (but not on airplanes), and a *gentleman* has a clean handkerchief. Weddings, funerals, and retirement speeches are usually occasions for the handkerchief. I just call these the business Boy Scout principles: be prepared.

- **Never Better Late.** You have heard the adage: "Better late than never." I say "Better never late." Set your watch five minutes fast and live on that time. Being habitually late is disrespectful. If you're on time, you're late. You are always walking to meetings down aisles and aisles of people. Everybody is watching you. So, I say, "Watch 'em back." Wave, stop to talk, compliment, pick up trash; any action that shows you are part of the team. You can't do those things if you are late for a meeting. I watched the GM of Ingersoll Rand go racing through their production floor and vowed never to be like that. Leave early for meetings to allow time for short visits along the way.

- **Humans are Hardwired for Stories.** People remember stories more than they remember facts and figures. That is just how our brains work. Sell your ideas with stories, anecdotes, and parables.

We all have different faiths, and I respect that, and I am amazed at how Jesus Christ never taught without using stories and illustrations. The head of a large pharmaceutical company was speaking at a Catawba College symposium. He told lots of stories. One was about his approach to their building maintenance staff. He said they were very good, but of course not perfect. He always made a specific comment about their cleaning, such as, there may have been a streak on the window, but overall, it was clean. His principle was, "It's better to be nice than right."

- **Good Manners Matter.** Learn and practice proper etiquette. I love the lyrics to the song "Humble and Kind," written by Lori McKenna and sung by Tim McGraw. If you are not familiar with the song, I suggest you look up the lyrics and reflect on the important message. Overcorrecting someone doesn't work. I remember when our vice president of sales, Benny Callahan, was inducted in the Catawba College Hall of Fame. He made an emotional acceptance speech. When he asked me what I thought I said, "Pretty good, but you said 'uh' forty-five times." I could see he was hurt and I felt terrible. I should have just been nice (sorry, Benny). Also, when I stay in a hotel room for more than one night, I make a point to leave a housekeeping tip the first night. It's just nice, and boy that room gets a lot of attention the rest of the stay. To me, it epitomizes the word TIPS: To Insure Prompt Service. A tip was originally meant to be paid in advance. That's what I practice on hotel stays.

My Mess-to-Success Story

How did I become an expert in communication skills? Let me assure you it was from listening to a great number of conversations, not from being born with these talents.

Let me share how I went from mess to success. In the early 1980s, I was lucky enough to get a job with the marketing department of Southern Alloy, a small metals company. Boy, was I lucky; but let's back up to the beginning.

Through high school and college, I always had a job of some kind: lawn mower, textile shipping clerk, stock boy, short order cook, dishwasher (hated that one), and brick packer (that was the hardest one).

The stock boy job at age thirteen was with Zimmerman's Department Store. The owners were (and still are) dear family friends. When I graduated from Catawba College, they hired me as their credit manager. Ugh! I spent my days approving credit cards and chasing bad debt. Yes, but owners Eddie Post and Leon Zimmerman gave me the chance to create marketing programs targeted to our 30,000 credit card holders. In hindsight, it was like running a business: branding, data mining, production, and ROI reporting. It was a terrific experience and prepared me for the biggest break of my life.

Mike Prillaman graduated from Catawba College with me. He worked at Southern Alloy and told me, "They like Catawba grads." I went to the interview wearing my best ugly brown three-piece suit with a torn sleeve shirt underneath. And I got the job. Thank you, Mike Prillaman.

The owner, Dick Virtue, told me and others at Southern Alloy, "If you ever want to run the company, it is my responsibility to help you do it."

The marketing department at Southern Alloy had unique approaches to sending out letters and doing database management. Other local companies, like our insurance agent, Bud Graeber, wanted to know what we were doing and how to do it. So Southern Alloy spun off the marketing department and made it into SOMAR (short for Southern Marketing), and Dick allowed me to become the manager.

My vision as manager was to one day run a successful company with 1,000 employees. That was the finish line for me. However, SOMAR was a miserable experiment for the first five years because we tried to be all things to all people. We were doing mailings, newspaper ads, and magazine advertisements.

We had no business being in business.

In 1987, Dick taught us about strategic planning. Dick allowed me to realize that SOMAR really had nothing going for it that would allow it to grow to 1,000 employees. No distinct competencies. No competitive advantage. No nothing. Well, except we had a computer the size of a coffee table that could dial phone numbers. Yep, at high speed, too.

"What's your plan?" asked Dick.

"Let's do one thing," I said, "do it better than anybody else, and do a lot of it."

That one thing happened to be telephone sales. Back in the late '80s, telephone sales were booming. SOMAR's strategy paid off, and we landed blue-chip telephone sales clients: First Union, Liberty Life, Discover Card, JCPenney, and Bank of America. Yes, doing one thing better than anybody else allowed us to boom. SOMAR went from two employees in 1986 to twenty employees in 1989, to 200 employees in 1991, and then to 2,000 employees in 1994.

Truth be known, SOMAR was workstation rich and cash poor at that point. But everybody in our industry in the late 1990s was going public, so we became part of a roll-up. Our company found a suitor, romanced developed, and SOMAR was bolted onto a company called Telespectrum out of Philadelphia. We went public, toasted our brilliance, and jumped on the public company roller-coaster. Dick Virtue was kind enough to make me a minority owner before the sale. So, the money was nice and paid the taxes on the cash and stock we received. *But*, the stock went way down, and our net proceeds were close to ten cents on the dollar.

Also, there was one hitch. I didn't want to work in Philadelphia. I grew up in Salisbury, North Carolina. I have a deep affinity for my hometown. So, when it came time to move to Philadelphia as president of the outbound division of Telespectrum, I declined.

Before I could launch my company GCS (Global Contact Services), I had to honor a four-year noncompete agreement from the sale of SOMAR. So I stayed out of the industry for that period of time.

Now, I believe in "grow where you're planted," so for GCS, we *got the band back together* in 2001 in Salisbury.

As a startup, GCS started from zero. It was another roller coaster ride, to say the least. For the first six years, we had issues such as the Do Not Call List, 9/11, and offshore competition. Despite the obstacles, GCS has grown to 1,000 employees in 2018, and our next goal is to quadruple in size.

At GCS, our differentiator is our ability to teach as many of our associates as possible about communications skills. That was the inspiration for this book. Because we're an audio business, holding conversations over the phone, we do the very best we can to be to make the most out of every single relationship. We want that for you, the reader, too.

Here is the aftermath of my story. The success of GCS over the last fifteen years has allowed me to balance my life with as many community efforts as possible. I work very closely with our church on being able to help with outreach programs. I served on the North Carolina State Board of Education, which has allowed my wife and me to help in the education field. We started an early childhood education nonprofit organization right here in Salisbury, devoted to preparing children ages zero to four to be ready for kindergarten so that they can be successful as they proceed in K–12. I'm on the board of trustees of my alma mater, Catawba College, and lead the finance committee. My other favorite boards include United Church Homes and Services, NC Early Childhood Foundation, Boy Scouts, Families First, Novant Rowan Foundation, First Tee of the Triad, and the Greg Alcorn Dishwashing Club. I do the dishes, cause nobody wants me to cook. Gotta know your limitations.

Where We Are Going

Part II of this book will cover how to overcome the seven biggest blunders. These blunders hold us back from success in business and in our personal lives. Our motto at GCS is, "Say this, not that." First, you need to notice the dumb things you are saying that are hurting you. Then you need to replace it with smart talk that will help you.

What to Say and How to Say It: Fixing Seven Common Blunders

SAY THIS	NOT THAT
Thank you for holding	Sorry you had to hold
Tell me your situation	What's your problem?
No wonder you are upset	Take it easy
Has this been helpful?	Guess we're done here
That must have really upset you	Take it easy; just be calm
May I put you on hold?	Hold, please
I'm researching now	Our system is slow today

"We are communicating better but we are still not out of the woods."

PART II

Say This, Not That

3

Beware of Your Bookends

From *A* to *Z*. The alpha and the omega. How you start and how you end.

Pay attention to your *conversation bookends*. These are the small comments or questions just before or right after a full statement or action. Stay tuned; we'll also talk about sentence bookends next.

Conversation bookends combined with proper and sincere voice inflection can make a good conversation great. In business, we say they lead to higher customer satisfaction. In your personal life, they will lead to better relationships.

But woe when they are done poorly.

The Case of the Just Curious Consultant

"Just curious."

That's the sentence bookend used by our client's consultant in New England. He drove everybody crazy by starting his barrage of questions with "Just curious." Really? How does curiosity morph into an hour of interrogating questions leading to nowhere?

"Just curious" became the nickname for the consultant. He couldn't help interrupting a planning session or a dashboard report meeting with a string of leading questions, starting with his signature sentence bookend. Sadly, the comment was a lie. Most poor sentence bookends are simply annoying or unnecessary. I'll share them next.

But here's more about Mr. Just Curious.

He liked to come in unannounced. A poster child for the "here I am" personality profile. He would list out demands for documentation of procedures and set unrealistic timeframes without consensus. He was both a joke and a threat. The client was brainwashed by this guy and jumped on board the "measure paperwork by the pound" boat.

To make it worse, his name, like mine, was Greg. Ugh. I spoke directly to him about our management team's irritation with his style but was not sure it made any difference. I don't know, because my short coaching session with him was at the end of our relationship. Thank goodness.

It's a tough recommendation to follow, but providing specific feedback to someone about their bookends is healthy. You can do it broadly to start with, but eventually, it's nice to make your feelings known. You also need to acknowledge your own flaws or "words to work on," too.

Here are some examples of sentence bookends we can all work on:

- Just asking…
- Just saying…
- Just curious…
- Wait; before you go any further…

- I'm confused...
- Not to get down in the weeds, but...
- Let me help *you* understand...
- To be clear...
- Here's something *you* didn't cover...
- So, let me put it differently...
- Do you have two seconds?
- Just a question...
- Is this a *bad* time?

Now, if Greg the Consultant would have cared, he could have crafted his "discovery phase" questions with *purposeful* sentence bookends: ones that created framework and teamwork. Bookends like:

- Is this a *good* time?
- Do you have about ten minutes?
- Can we compare notes on this process?
- I need *your* help...
- I have *several* questions for you...
- My report will include...
- The recommendations are due Friday; when is a good time to...
- I want your thoughts on a potential improvement.

Conversation bookends balance the technical and the personal in a relationship. When employed correctly, bookends frame the facts and the feelings of a relationship. They merge subject matter with empathy.

They match *what* you say with *how* you say it for mutual benefit. They're cool. I'm *not* just sayin'.

And, yes, I'm trying to eliminate the word "just" from my vocabulary.

The First and Last Are Most Important

Good conversation bookends can keep the temperament of the person you are speaking with productive and professional. You want the conversation to be on the right path. Bad bookends can send the conversation into the ditch.

Now, let's cover sentence bookends. These are those one-word intros or single word endings to your comment or question. They can range from powerful to annoying. Truth is, we often don't realize when we use them. For illustration, a Valley Girl persona says the word "like" a lot. (I know, like, I don't even have to give, like, an example.)

Here is the bookend rule of thumb: Sentence bookends are good to use occasionally to engage the other person. Bookends are bad to use frequently. This is when bookends are perceived as annoying.

Here are some pre-sentence bookends to avoid, especially if you use them habitually to start every sentence:

- So
- You know
- All right
- Well

- Listen
- Just
- Now
- No

These starting bookends, when used constantly, are hurting you. In most cases, you can replace these words with a pause, a moment of silence between sentences.

Good and Bad Bookends

Bookends are just a tool like electricity is a tool. And like any tool, they can be used for helping or for harming. Electricity can cook a person's dinner, or it can cook a person. Bookends can turn people on or turn people off.

Pre-sentence bookends as a tool can be engaging, demeaning, or distracting. Names are great bookends. Starting a sentence with the name of the person you are talking to warms that person up. "Mary, may I put you on hold?" Saying your name last in your introduction makes it easy for the person you are talking with remember your name. "This is the helpline; my name is Jack."

But what if you use a name to start or end *every* sentence? "Jack, tell me your situation. Let's check your account, Jack. Jack, I'm researching now." *Overuse* of names is just *creepy*.

Use phrases with the person you are talking with that will build a partnership. Do this by asking permission and talking through the upcoming steps. "May I ask, is there anything else we can do to help?"

Avoid negative bookends. Negative words add to customers' discomfort. They also hurt in social situations. Starting or ending with "sorry" is not a bookend that will help you. A great bookend is "thank you." Compare these two bookends: "Thank you for holding" versus "Sorry you had to hold."

The TV show *Saturday Night Live* once featured a character called Debbie Downer, played by Rachel Dratch. Debbie used bad bookends that depressed all around her. "You know who likes Christmas? Credit card companies."

And from children's literature, we have the A.A. Milne *Winnie the Pooh* character Eeyore, the sad sack donkey. "I should have known" and "Don't blame me if it rains" are typical Eeyore bookend comments.

Mind your bookends, so you are not a Debbie Downer or an Eeyore.

Right? Right? Right? Wrong

Post-sentence bookends can be nice affirmations. Unfortunately, they are often used by the speaker to hog the conversation and continue talking.

Once a client finished fourteen consecutive sentences with the question, "Right?" It sounded something like this:

"You don't correct your largest client, right? If your largest client's clothes don't match, you don't mention it, right? If your largest client uncomfortably cusses inappropriately, you just go along, right?"

PRINCIPLE

One of the most annoying sentence bookends is "right?" To me, saying, "right?" repetitively at the end of *every* sentence is a form of conversational bullying. Sure, it's OK when used as a sincere question and followed by listening. But when used to just continue talking, it's wrong. When used to force affirmation, it's very wrong. When used to convince and lead to another viewpoint, it's *extremely* wrong.

It goes like this: "You want to make money, right? So, I can help you with that by building a strategy to monetize your value proposition, right? You need the best resources to make money fast and in the long run, right? Everybody wants that, right? That's why you have me, right? I'll help you after we finish the consulting paperwork and started, right now!"

Excuse me, I don't recall agreeing to go down that path. And now the conversation is in the ditch.

Lesson learned: Only answer "Right?" with "Yes, that's correct," if you really mean it. Oh, and don't say "Right" when the driver asked if he should turn left.

Here are some other post-sentence bookends to be wary of:

- OK?
- You know?

- Am I right?
- You got it?
- Know what I mean?
- You with me here?
- Follow what I am saying?
- Don't you agree?
- Does that make sense to you?

Asking questions is a good tool. Just don't overuse it. An honest "Do you agree that..." used sparingly can be a great bookend. The trick is, you need to honestly listen to what the other person has to say. That is just respect.

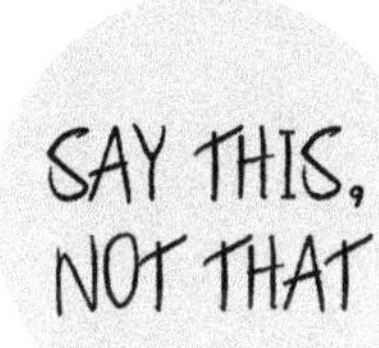

Beware Your Bookends

SAY THIS	NOT THAT
Mary, thank you for holding	Hello? Are you still there?
May I ask a favor?	Please hold, back in a sec
OK if I look up your account?	Let me see what we have on you
I have three questions, and one comment	Let's talk

"What if, and I know this sounds kooky, we communicated with the employees."

Focus on First Few Words

Be prepared with your first three words (or two or four—let's not quibble). My son is an Eagle Scout. So, the whole Boy Scout motto, "Be prepared," is on my brain a lot.

When our first company, SOMAR, had its explosive growth spurt in '94-'95, we hired more than 1,000 employees in West "by God" Virginia. We opened centers in Beckley, Charleston, and Huntington. This got the attention of the Governor's office and lots of other politicians.

At every opening, there was lots of fanfare. The announcements got bigger and more interesting as we canvassed the state. West Virginia had double-digit unemployment during both expansions. The state also had *under*employment. West Virginians are loyal and family-oriented, so even with college degrees and few job prospects, they like to stay in their home state. At every opening, we had three to five times more qualified applicants than positions. We love West Virginia.

I had a standard speech for each stop: appreciation, our culture, our long-term commitment to communities, and back to appreciation. The speech contained some humor, recognized key decision-makers, brought out a human-interest story, and closed strong. It was great. But something happened with the other speakers at almost every stop.

In Beckley, the president of Bell Atlantic (now Verizon) stumbled through his announcement during a lunchtime presentation. Next, I did my standard speech. That evening, that same president made one of the best speeches of the trip. He upped his game once he knew how important the day was becoming.

In Charleston, we spent about an hour behind closed doors with Governor Caperton. He was hilarious. He's married to the conductor of the New York City Philharmonic and told a story on himself. When a reporter asked him why the SOMAR parade went through the fancy part of town, Caperton said, "If you're touring New York, you don't go through Harlem, do you?" Then the Governor made a huge animated lunge and outstretched his hand. "I was trying to grab those words back. I knew they would be trouble." And they made media headlines, but he survived and served two terms.

In Huntington, we had a parade with the Marshall University marching band and probably the biggest crowd we'd ever had. The mayor, Jean Dean (yep, that's her real name), was with us all day. It had been a warm day, and we had a late dinner with more than 200 people and more speeches. Mayor Dean started to make her nighttime proclamation on stage and immediately *fainted*. Boom, right to the floor at my feet. Of course, we were shocked. The EMTs were right outside, got her comfortable, and headed home.

Guess who was next on the program? I started my speech, which I'm sure nobody heard because we were still worried about the mayor. Fortunately, her husband came back into the room to let us know she was fine. The full day, the heat, the packed schedule, and no food had caused the episode. She fully recovered and was back to normal the next day. We love Mayor Dean.

In 2004, we did the whole thing again as GCS. This time, we built centers near Beckley, Huntington, and (this time around) Wheeling, near Pittsburgh.

By the time we reopened in Beckley, there was a new governor, Bob Wise. We had the grand opening of our showcase GCS center in 2002. The event was held outdoors, and it was windy. We had to wait about an hour for the governor, who arrived by helicopter. During my speech, a gust of wind blew over a huge audio speaker from its tripod. The speaker was the size of a dishwasher and narrowly missed hitting Benny Callahan, our number one salesperson, on the head. Benny was responsible for such accounts as Discover Card, Sears, JCPenney, and AIG. When I recognized him in my speech, I meant to say he was equivalent to basketball's Michael Jordan in our industry. Instead, I slipped and said he was the Michael *Jackson* of our industry. What a Thriller.

Be prepared, right? Just like an Eagle Scout.

Your First Few Words

I cannot overemphasize the importance of a first impression. The first impression is not just the first time you meet somebody, it's the first time you meet somebody at any time.

Take, for example, the question, "How are you?" Is this asked rhetorically, or are you truly interested in the other person? If you are sincerely interested, that comes through your voice. This is important at home and at work.

Another approach to the first three words is to recognize the number one word to every single person is his or her *name*. So, being able to use that as part of your first three words is powerful. Did you ever see a child light up when you're in a room with thirty people, mostly adults, when you say "Hey, Maggie!" Being able to address people by their name goes a long way.

Using names is important when speaking on the phone, especially conference calls. Conference call principle number one is if you're going to call on somebody, start with the name. Instead of saying, "What were the metrics on our operations yesterday, Frank?" ask the right way: "Frank, what were the metrics on our operation yesterday?" If you don't start with the name, you might catch the person by surprise. It certainly catches people's attention when you say their name first. Even in introductions, you can't go wrong with saying the person's name first.

Four Powerful Words

A person's name followed by the four words "I need your help" is a winner. "Rachel, I need your help."

This is especially powerful when it's in a situation in which you might be the boss, and the other person might be a manager, or you might be in a perceived superior position.

In sports, if the coach goes to a player and says, "Frank, I need your help," that creates a different dynamic than a coach chewing the player out. If the boss says, "Leon, I need your help," this creates a positive situation.

"I need your help" can defuse difficult situations.

The first few words set the stage from a mental, emotional, and attitudinal standpoint. The first few words can frame it. What you never want is to frame the exchange as an adversarial conversation. This puts people on the defensive. "You probably don't know this answer, but I'll ask you anyway." Really? What's the upside to starting a question with a demeaning intro? None.

I Trust You

When people are on the defensive, they never do their best work. In January of 2006, a computer virus attack shut down our company completely for four days. When Bob Dunmire, our vice president of technology, told me of the problem, the first three words I told him were, "I trust you."

That's *all* I said. Actually, it was by email. Bob said it changed his life. Three little words typed from a remote mountain house on the day our company was *paralyzed* by a computer virus. Our business in 2006 had 2,000 employees that *relied* on 800 desktop computers making two million customer contacts a month. We were dead in the water. Revenue per *day* went from $100,000 to *zero*.

For the next week, our Information Tech team traveled to all thirteen sites, wiping the virus off of every computer. We were back up and running because of their heroic efforts. No clocks, no complaints: our team fixed it. Our clients understood. We survived.

Never underestimate the power of truly empowering words communicated at the right time. It made me feel great that Bob felt great. It is like when somebody says, "You've made my day." Heck, they make *your* day.

Two More Weeks

With that virus in mind, let's consider three words *not to say.*

Did you see the '80s Tom Hanks movie called *Money Pit,* about a young married couple renovating an older home? The contractor's answer to every question about how long any project would take was, "Two more weeks." Two weeks later, when the contractor would be asked it the project was finished, he would answer, no: "Two more weeks."

I don't mind mistakes or delays as long as they're communicated and as long as they're the exception rather than the rule. I used to take my car to a repair shop that was always behind. The shop did good work, but the inconvenience wasn't worth the craftsmanship. Changing oil and getting an inspection should not require asking favors of family and friends to provide unanticipated transportation.

If you talk to most businesspeople who have had long-term relationships with a vendor, they always point to the crisis or problem that they worked through.

In our ten years of operation, we have only had that one computer virus. We communicated openly with our clients, and they appreciated that the virus was controlled, quarantined, and caused no permanent damage. We tried to follow the rules of good customer service when things go wrong: make sure you communicate and make sure it doesn't happen again. Oh, and make sure the fix doesn't take *two more weeks.*

Sometimes twenty minutes can feel liked two more weeks, as this story demonstrates.

Account Number, Please?

"Account number, please?"

Those three words sent customers ballistic.

The CEO of a major technology company (let's call him Mr. Jones) was irritated because his engineers wound up fixing systems that were integrated with competitors' systems (thanks to Chris Stiehl, author of *Pain Killer Marketing,* for this true cautionary tale with some names changed to protect privacy).

Sometimes when the overall system failed, his engineers had to fix the competitor's problem in order to make the overall system perform, or the client would not purchase the warranty coverage required for repairs. His engineers would just diagnose these problems and fix them.

Mr. Jones did not like fixing problems that were out of warranty or involved a competitor's product. He decreed at a meeting of all the corporate VPs that this practice had to stop!

It turned out that the top 125 customers in the world for Mr. Jones' company were all given a special telephone number to call when their systems failed. For many of these customers, they would be losing $1 million per minute or more while down.

Because of Mr. Jones' decree, these customers began to be screened when they called. Mr. Jones' customer advocates asked questions like, "Account number, please?" and, "Can you tell me the contract number under which you purchased the piece of equipment that failed, the part number that failed, and whether or not you purchased warranty coverage for repairs to that equipment if it failed?"

For these huge customers, answering such questions could take fifteen to twenty minutes or more dealing with a customer advocate before a caller ever spoke to an engineer to start diagnosing and fixing the problem. Mr. Jones' most important customers were losing millions of dollars talking to a customer advocate rather than getting their systems repaired. The advocates were being measured based upon how much money they saved in repair costs to Mr. Jones' company. The engineers who were diagnosing and solving customer problems were being measured on how quickly they repaired the customer's system *once they were given permission to work on the problem*. The clock for the engineers did not start until they were assigned the problem to solve by a customer advocate.

When Stiehl was asked to work on complaints by these major customers by Mr. Jones, the solution was obvious (at least to Stiehl). The tech company was not thinking like its customers were thinking. When did the customer's clock start? The moment his or her system went down, of course—well before the moment the engineer started working on the problem. Thus, complaints.

Stiehl advised Mr. Jones to make his metric line up with the customer metric. If he needed to send a bill later for repairing the customer's system, Stiehl was sure these customers would pay it, given the amount of money involved.

When this was explained to Mr. Jones and his team, they were embarrassed to be saving proverbial pennies in their own costs of repairing customer systems while the customers were losing big time. With an appropriate focus—putting the customer needs first—they were able to gain tremendously in goodwill and the trust of their major customers, regardless of whose problem was being fixed.

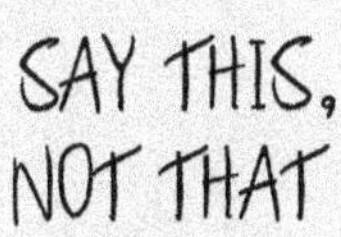

Focus on First Few Words

SAY THIS	NOT THAT
I need your help	We need to talk
Share your thought process	Why did you do that?
Help me out	What were you thinking?
I trust you	Better convince me
Help me clarify	I don't believe you
Let's *fix it*	We got big trouble
Let's find the root cause	I'm confused

JUST FYi... SO FAR YOUR OVERALL COMMUNiCATiON SCORES ARE PRETTY DiSMAL! ...DO GO ON!
Bill Whitehead

5

Choose Your Words Well

"Clichés and cussing are forms of mental illness."

I first read that in the Tom Robbins novel *Skinny Legs and All*. In the book, two characters are talking, and one uses a cliché, such as, "If it's not one thing, it's another." The other character claims that clichés are a form of avoidance. He says clichés are a way to not state your true thoughts or feelings.

Same with cussing, and I think that's bullshit.

After I read the Robbins book, I begin noticing one of our sales guys filled his weekly updates with clichés. These clichés were mostly baseball analogies, such as "I'm just swinging the bat," and "It's a game of numbers, and I'm due to get some hits."

"How many appointments do you have scheduled?" I would ask.

"I'm taking it one game at a time," he would say.

"I don't give a damn about baseball right now." I began to stoop to the cliché-and-cussing level.

Now I listen very closely to our new sales people for clichés and I try not to cuss.

I don't swear just for the hell of it.

PRINCIPLE

When you use clichés, don't mistake them for wisdom.

Picking the Right Words

"Repeat." That one word is all it took to double the sales of a shampoo. It is not just "lather and rinse." It's *lather, rinse, repeat*. Brilliant.

Choosing your words well starts with your attention towards *intention*. You can look at something negatively, or you can look at it positively. You can look at it optimistically, or you can look at it pessimistically. Is your shop open until five or do you close at five? You will be surprised how simple word selection affects attitude.

Word selection makes an enormous difference in the listener's attitude and perception. I'm amazed at the negative approach to the smallest detail, such as *Use Other Door*. What's up with that? Put a more positive spin to promote using the unlocked door. How about *Use This Door*? That way, the person seeing the sign only must think about *one* door, and that's the one to open.

We naturally like to hang around people who are interesting. We also gravitate toward people who are interested in *us.* The same goes for word selection. Interesting words and terms can give comfort, show benefits, and just make us feel better.

Which would you rather buy, a *used* car or a car that is *certified pre-owned*?

(How about "Pontiac builds excitement?" Let's buy some certified pre-owned *excitement*. Sounds like a second marriage. OK, maybe that is going too far, but do you see the point?)

The message is that word selection matters.

A great way to overcome the blunder of poor word choice is to build a glossary of positive, benefit-oriented terms. Simply make your own. You'll be surprised at how your perception of the world can improve. (How did the Europeans come up with *water closet* for a toilet? I like it.)

Here are some word choices in my negative-to-positive glossary:

- Discipline or write-up could be *performance improvement plan.*
- Monitoring could be *coaching.*
- Closed Sunday could be *Open Monday to Saturday.*
- Waiting room could be *reception area.*

Why Master Word Selection?

There are four benefits of mastering word selection.

1. Your words express your attitude and your personality. People view your more favorably when you use positive words.

2. Using positive terms is contagious. Your customers and coworkers are much more comfortable and can focus on the task.

3. You earn higher customer satisfaction scores (even with a *family member*). Our data clearly demonstrates this. Customers score you mainly from how they feel following your conversation (the same holds true for personal conversations). Remember that it's not just what you say, it is *how you say it.*

4. Positive communications make your day go faster. You feel better about your work and life. That gives you more energy, too.

The FAB Formula is Your Friend

When choosing words, it pays to keep the *FAB Formula* in mind. FAB stands for Features/Advantages/Benefits.

There are three ways to describe a product or service:

- **Features.** Features are key characteristics (often, but not always, physical) that make up a product or service. If you are talking about a car, you might say the car is red. The color is a feature.
- **Advantages.** The advantages are the performance characteristics. This is the way the product or service acts or performs. The advantage of a red car is it is easy to spot (the disadvantage is it is easy to spot by state troopers on the highway, but that is another story).

- **Benefits.** The benefits are the personal characteristics—how the product or service impacts your lifestyle. A red car that is easy to spot gets you noticed (hopefully in a positive way).

So, it pays to plan what you say.

PRINCIPLE

Another way to think of the FAB formula is:

What it is—What it does—Why we like it

People value things based on how they perceive them to make a difference in their lives. Typically, the more valuable the benefits for the customer, the more they value the product. This chart provides examples to illustrate:

ITEM	FEATURE	ADVANTAGE	BENEFIT
Water treatment	Clean water	Water from the tap	Health
Refuse pickup	Every Monday	Curbside service	Clean city
Police department	Police officers	Deters crime	Preserves property
Pothole repair	Full-time team	Gets fixed quickly	Reduced car damage
Health plan	Insurance	Coverage	Peace of mind

Using the FAB Formula is a great way to reinforce the benefits of the products and/or services you provide. This works on a personal level, too. Often, we need to seek assistance from mates, family, and friends. When you can tie what you are talking about to personal benefits, then you often raise the value to the listener.

Words Drive Behaviors

Consider this: *Words drive behavior, and behavior drives results.*

Please recall the best teachers and coaches you have had in your life. These are the people who made you feel good and learn better. Most likely they used positive, benefit-oriented words directed straight at you. Copy their words and behaviors, and better results will follow.

Compare the words of a coach versus a fan. Coaching terms are those that emphasize an activity, whereas fans emphasize a result.

So, in basketball terms, fans yell, "Get the rebound! We have to get this rebound."

The coach is not using those words. The coach says, "Box out, stay in your position, keep your arms out, and keep your elbows out. It's a zone, so make sure your obligations are to the big five and the four."

That's the way a coach talks. And that's why, if you're coaching somebody, you should pick the words that are behavior- or activity-based, as opposed to results-based. Because we only control our behaviors; we can't control the result. In a later chapter, there is a perfect example of this coaching process: the Lisa James story.

Make people feel glad as much as possible, sad when necessary, and mad when they need to be. Sometimes you may even choose words to make people scared, if urgency is required, such as, "There's a *fire* in the kitchen!"

Ifs, Ands, But no Buts

Mark Twain said, "The difference between the *almost right word* and the *right word* is really a large matter. 'Tis the difference between the lightning bug and the lightning."

If is a right word. Starting a sentence with the right word can be uplifting. The word *if* is a word of possibility.

But is an almost right word. The word *but*, as opposed to *if*, is deflating. Say you give someone a compliment, such as, "You look nice today" or, "You handled that presentation well." Now, if you replace the period in those sentences with a comma and then add the word *but*, everything before the comma is forgotten.

"Frank, you did a really good job yesterday, but I think the expenses in that operation are way out of control." So, what do you hear? *Expenses are way out of control.*

The right word you are looking for is *and*.

Say this instead: "Frank you did a really great job yesterday, and we need to talk about how to get expenses down." Now Frank hears the praise and the concern.

This is an even better approach: "Frank, you did a great job yesterday. What'd you think?"

And let him go through it. Hopefully, he says, "Thanks, Greg. We still need to get expenses down."

So, if Frank can beat you to the punch about bringing up the expense issue, then Frank is much more open to being coached on that topic.

What words might the boss use?

"Frank, I've got some ideas on expenses, and I want to hear yours first." Hopefully, when you get to the end of his list, you can say, "Great, you got all the ideas I was thinking about."

PRINCIPLE

Get the *buts* out of your mouth and use *and* instead. Saying *but* negates everything that you previously said. A compliment that includes the word *but* is no compliment at all. Keep compliments and evaluations in separate silos.

Check Your Mirrors

I check my side mirrors before I back up. Sounds routine. Something you learn in driver's education.

Yet one time I didn't and paid for it. For my first traveling sales job with Southern Alloy, I had a small, four-door, company car that I parked in a tight garage: a silver, VW Rabbit, nicknamed Bullet. One morning, I put my bag in the back seat, started the car, and backed out of the garage. Suddenly there was a loud noise and to my left was the back door. I had failed to close the car's back door, and it was now buckled and bent almost to the rearview mirror. Boy, did I feel stupid.

The hard part was telling my boss. I felt so low and disappointed with myself and couldn't imagine how I had done such a dumb thing. I also had to prepare myself for some real discipline, financial responsibility, and maybe even getting fired.

I went to my boss, told him the story, and waited for his response, which I predicted would be an explosion. He looked at me and said, "No problem. It was an accident. Get it fixed. That's what insurance is for. Now, when will you have the inventory completed?"

Inventory completed? Really?

My boss knew I was feeling bad and he knew I understood my responsibility, so he didn't need to teach me any lesson at that moment. So he took the positive, supportive route and totally changed my outlook.

PRINCIPLE

OK, we have a problem. No need to pile on. Now be part of the solution. Go get it fixed. That's right; *fix it!*

Another principle I learned from that boss was "Show the emotion you want them to see." I felt terrible, and he had the experience to know the car could be fixed later, so let's focus on fixing Greg now. It worked. I had the inventory done in record time, worked till 7:30 p.m. that night, and was ready to run through walls for my boss upon command.

Months later, we would laugh at that morning's events, and coworkers would pantomime just how hard it was for me to walk around the back door of the car without closing it. But that morning, my boss took a positive approach to a negative situation, and it really made my day. And, yes, I still check my mirrors to look for other cars, animals, and open rear car doors.

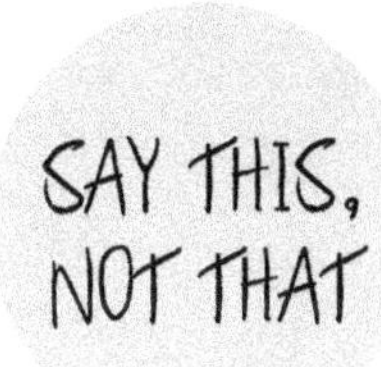

Choose Your Words Well

SAY THIS	NOT THAT
Sanitation worker	Garbage man
Customer advocates	Call takers
Coverage	Insurance
Children	Kids
Police officers	Cops
You're welcome	No problem
I hear you	Go on

"You've always been a poor listener Harold."

6

Ask Questions and Master Listening

The late Stephen Covey, author of the mega-selling personal-organization books, such as *The 7 Habits of Highly Effective People*, laid out homespun principles. Some personal favorites were "Be proactive" and "Put first things first."

Of the seven habits, my favorite is the fifth: "Seek first to understand, then to be understood."

Here's the college-level reasoning: Use empathic listening to be genuinely interested in a person, which allows them the freedom to reciprocate the listening and have an open mind to being influenced by you. This creates an atmosphere of caring, respect, and positive problem-solving.

Boil it down, and you end up with the Golden Rule: treat others as *you* want to be treated (although I am also a fan of author Tony Alessandra's Platinum Rule: treat others as *they* want to be treated),

Our approach to customer service can be characterized by empathic listening, influence, and positive problem-solving. So, when it comes to customer service, our clients benefit from our approach.

For example, our insurance agents are highly skilled in giving examples of unexpected situations in which our insurance products can protect a family's financial well-being. Our Eastwood City BPO group can quickly verify education and employment history for large data warehouses. Also, our folks in Yuma, Arizona are bilingual and can toggle between English and Spanish to match the customer's first language.

The theme of these three examples is to first understand the customer and then respond to their situation. Sounds like the Golden Rule to me.

Listen to Complaints

A rose by any other name is still a rose, according to Shakespeare. A complaint, however, by another name can be an opportunity. Complaints come in many forms. Forms such as valid, invalid, minor, major, resolvable, irresolvable, an excuse, avoidance, a lie, a response to an untruth or exaggeration, or just a cry for help.

Complaints are often a crossroad in a relationship. They can either improve the relationship or discontinue the relationship. Sometimes to discontinue is the best alternative, following the Native American Dakota principle, "When one finds oneself riding a dead horse, the best alternative is to dismount." In our business, customer care and service programs sometimes include handling complaints. Someone calls to cancel their membership because they don't see the value connected to the annual fee. That's a valid complaint, usually minor, and potentially resolvable. Our job is to explain the value and let the customer decide if the fee is justifiable, with no lies or exaggerations; just facts, feelings and civil questions and responses. Regardless of the decision by the customer, the goal is to make sure the experience is a pleasant one.

A couple years ago, we had a client who complained all the time. She even went so far as telling us her complaining was deliberate and was her way of getting the best results. After about three months, we fired the client. Life is too short for energy-draining, negative relationships.

The best complaints are the ones that improve a relationship. These complaints are really stating a concern. Someone cares about you enough to point out a concern because they value the relationship and want it to last. I have a pet peeve about eating habits, for example, and don't mind *complaining* to my family or coworkers when basic manners can be improved.

Recently we had a client complain about us reallocating the resources used for their programs. It was a valid concern, and I was very appreciative to hear their feelings. We had a face-to-face meeting to discuss the past, present, and future of their programs, and the relationship is now at an all-time high.

A rose is always a rose, but a complaint is oftentimes an opportunity.

PRINCIPLE

Complaints are opportunities—opportunities to fix, improve, and grow. The only thing you want to avoid with complaints is to hear the same one twice. There is nothing more energy draining than the continuous drone of repeated complaints. We must take advantage of the opportunity embedded in complaints and resolve them the first time.

Dealing With Rejection

"When you are told, 'No', it is for one of three reasons," said the seminar leader. "An excuse, a resolvable reason, or an irresolvable reason."

The seminar teacher at the front of the room I was sitting in gave several examples and taught us how to ask clarifying questions to determine pursue or quit. (I wish I'd learned these techniques when dating; It would have helped with all the rejections.)

Another topic was identifying the emotional level we hear or say by the voice tone. The three levels were Parent, Adult, and Child. The Parent had a subset: Nurturing parent and Critical parent. The Child had subsets as well: Natural child, Rebellious child and Accepting child. We would role-play conversations and try to identify the emotional level each participate was intending to send through his or her vocal tone versus how it was received. How many different ways can you say "be careful"?

My favorite topic in the seminar was body language. How many times have you watched a person from across the room and could instantly tell if he or she was happy, sad, or angry? Facial expressions, nods, acknowledgments, hand and leg positions, eye contact: all can make or break a conversation. You can greatly affect the emotional direction of a conversation by displaying the right body language. When I want to make a point during a meeting, I might stand up, lean forward, or smile, using active language with my arms extended and palms open. Think of Joel Osteen, the televangelist based in Houston.

I took that seminar more than twenty-five years ago, and the principles still apply today. Improving our emotional intelligence includes a lifetime of experiences, lessons, and applied learning. When it comes to learning how to deal with people, it's better to be nurturing and natural than critical and rebellious. It's better to be nice than right.

World-Class Listening

Being a world-class listener requires thought to be able to manifest the behavior. Of course, it also requires a great amount of practice.

Once you're conscious of listening, it is very rewarding. In sales, you should be talking 25 percent of the time. That means you're asking questions and the prospect is doing most of the talking. Listen to the prospect tell you what they want to buy.

I believe world-class listening can be improved by focusing on four areas brought to you by Bell Leadership.

1. **Commit.** The number one thing is to commit. Just make a conscious commitment to being a great listener. That goes a long way. Asking for peer support is a sign of your commitment. Get a buddy to listen to you. Get feedback on how you can do better as a listener. Think parallel monologues vs. dialogues.

2. **To Be or Not to Be.** The second area is Shakespeare's Hamlet's focus in his "To be or not to be" speech. This is like shooting free throws in basketball. The best free-throw shooters make baskets 90 percent of the time. If you're average, you make baskets 75 percent of the time. To improve requires focus. Same with listening. It is up to you if it is going to be or not to be. In our circle, we all have permission to be able to say, "I'm sorry; I wasn't even close to listening." You don't have to fake it. You know what it's like when you're sitting there staring at somebody, and they're talking, and you're looking right past them, and you're thinking about dinner or what's on TV tonight. Then they ask you what you think, and it's like, "Whoops, I just wasn't listening." Better to stay in the game and choose to listen.

3. **Ask World-Class Questions.** You need to know the difference between two things that are basic, and that's to know the difference between a closed-ended question and an open-ended question. Closed-ended questions have one-word or single-phrase answers. Did you see the game last night? Great, wasn't it? What was the score?

What color is that shirt? What time did you wake up this morning? Those are all questions that just lead to *instant answers.* Open-ended questions require more elaborate answers. What did you do last night? After they answer, you can say, "Tell me about it," "Fill me in," or, "How'd it go?" If you still want to stick with sports, that's fine. Try "What'd you think of the defense in the game last night?" or "So, is Xball your favorite sport or is there another that really gets you going?" If they sound uncomfortable, don't probe. But 99 percent of the time, people *like* talking about their interests. And you learn something. The same techniques get people talking and keep them talking about business problems.

4. **Take Notes.** You can call this one as corny and as old school as you could ever find, but it's taking notes. If you write it down, it's harder to forget it. So, if you're going to be a world-class listener, write down what somebody says. Not only does it help you remember, equally as important is that you can later *use the words that they use* in the conversation. This builds rapport. If they call their car Old Betsy, you should refer to the car as Old Betsy. Be sure to note other specifics like names and numbers. There is an adage that the weakest ink is stronger than the best memory. If you say you are going to get back to Larry at 5:00 p.m. Tuesday and you write in your notes, "Get back to Larry by 5:00 p.m. Tuesday," it is much more likely to happen.

Want to Learn to Be a Better Listener?

There are other courses on listening. There are even conferences about listening.

The International Listening Association (ILA) is an organization developed to promote the study, development, and teaching of listening. The association is "dedicated to learning more about the impact that listening has on all human activity." The ILA was founded in 1979 In Minneapolis, Minnesota, USA. The ILA holds annual conferences that include people of varied backgrounds related to listening to provide a full range of interesting perspectives on listening. Presenters include communication professors, corporate trainers, audiologists, musicians, researchers, and more. Or, check out Bell Leadership in Chapel Hill, NC.

What do great listeners have in common? They show a greater interest in others than in themselves in communications. How to develop an attitude like that is the focus of the following chapter.

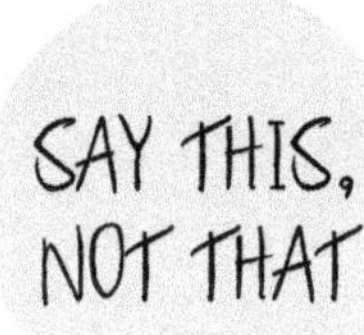

Ask Questions and Master Listening

SAY THIS	NOT THAT
Tell me more	I can top that
Tell me your backstory	How long have you done your job?
What's your story?	Where are you from?
Start from the beginning	When did you meet?
Tell me about him/her	How old is he/she?

YES, I'M COACHING THIS WORKSHOP. COME IN, YOU STUPID IDIOT!

7

More You, Less Me Attitude

He was an All-American football player. He was Rowan County's Athlete of the Year in the mid-1980s. As far as I know, he still holds the record for Division III kickoff and punt return yardages.

That's Bryan Overcash. Now here is the unusual part of the story: I learned about his athletic prowess about three years *after* he became our VP of Finance. Three whole years.

Now, it took me about three hours to tell *him* about *my* legendary career in Little League baseball. I also was quick to share my storied college basketball career, which lasted a total of two weeks before quitting.

I was on the Cinderella UNC-Charlotte basketball team that made it to the Final Four and barely lost to Marquette. I scored the first basket in the first intersquad game. A few days after that epic layup (and about ten turnovers), I was called to the coaches' office. Coach Pratt kindly told me I was the seventeenth man on the seventeen-man roster, and the sixteenth guy was player of the year in his home state. He said I would rarely play, if ever, not travel on away games, probably not even play in practice, but I could stay on the team if I wished. Yes, I quit. I joined an intramural team and watched those sixteen guys make history.

Now, look at that previous paragraph. Who's it about? *Me, myself, and I.* Did I mention this book is about the dumb things we all say, including me? Yes, I have made my share.

Why are we like this? Why can't we wait to tell our story, no matter how trivial? What's worse is not asking for a similar story from someone like Bryan. His story is far more exciting and intriguing to me because *I already know my story. More Bryan and Less Greg* is a good attitude reminder for Greg.

Also, note that Bryan's humility is so genuine and real, he would have *never* told me of his Top 1 Percent career. The only way I learned this was by visiting his house and seeing the trophies, pictures, and articles. Now I tell everybody about *him.*

I've known Bryan for decades, and he's the epitome of *More You, Less Me.* His conversation bookends are time-management-principle-based. "I have three questions and one request," starts his meeting. He goes to lunch and offers to get me something. He sees the trash being taken out and rushes to help. He changes his doctor's appointment (bad knee, and now you know why) to attend an important client meeting. He's a *you* guy.

Oh, and he probably asked me ten questions during my somewhat hyped-up version of my Little League story. Who else hit fourteen home runs in twelve games, batted .678, and pitched two no-hitters? Whoops, there I go again. In one no-hitter, I walked seven guys and hit two. I was one wild and crazy pitcher. "*OK, enough about me; what do* you *think about me?*"

Let Bryan tell you. He's now our chief operating officer and partner in the ownership of our company.

On Being Selfish Vs. Selfless

Are you selfish or selfless? Most of us don't even know.

The people we warm up to are those who give us comfort in their attitude. What kind of attitude do you want to have? I want people to know that I am caring and that I have a passion for what I'm doing.

There are times when it is important to be selfish. We need to make sure we're taking care of ourselves because the physical part of our life is the foundation for everything else. That has been called *sacred selfishness* because we need to make sure we are eating right, getting enough sleep, and getting proper exercise. If you don't feel good, or if you have limitations based on that physical part of life, that potentially can hinder your ability to serve others.

That kind of selfishness is a minor part of your life. If you can be perceived as *selfless* in most of your life, then you're in pretty good shape.

The same is true in conversations. Taking care of your needs in the conversation should be the minor part. The major part of conversation should be selfless. This comes down to the *questions* that you ask, the amount of time we focus on *listening*, and the types of *bookends* you use.

The attitude aspect that resonates first with me is how you enter a room. Are you the person who walks into a room and says, "Here I am," or are you the one who walks in and says, "There you are"?

Think about that difference. People whose entrance says "Here I am" are typically about themselves. They're more interested in what they're doing. They want everybody to recognize them. The opposite are people who walk in the room, and nobody even knows they have arrived. They're there to be able to help and work with everybody else. A "there you are" person is there to give. A "here I am" person wants to take the spotlight.

So, watch your words. Do you use the words *me*, *myself*, and *my* more than you use the words *you*, *yours*, and *ours*? Note the subtle difference between "I want to thank you for inviting me" and "thank you for inviting me." In the first sentence, there is an *I attitude*, versus the second sentence, which has a *you attitude*.

Remember your grammar school teacher drilling into you that the sentence should be "Mary and I went to the store," not "Me and Mary went to the store"? That is not only good grammar, it is also placing people in the right order and displaying the right attitude.

Motivation vs. Inspiration

Attitude is a pillar of motivation. Inspiration is external; it is when you emotionally gain something from somebody else. Motivation is internal. Motivation is your motor because it's what you want to do.

A lot of that internal attitude happens with positive self-talk.

Here is a definition of self-talk from the website for the magazine *Psychology Today.*

> *Cheerful and supportive or negative and self-defeating, this internal chatter is referred to as "self-talk." Your self-talk combines your conscious thoughts with your unconscious beliefs and biases. It's an effective way for your brain to interpret and process your daily experience. However, human nature is prone to negative self-talk, making sweeping assertions like "I can't do anything right!" or "I'm a complete failure!" We know this negativity can be unrealistic or even harmful, but we do it anyway. The good news is that you can learn to challenge that negative self-talk, and the first step is becoming more aware of it.*[1]

Self-talk, when done right, is self-coaching to help with your attitude. When you are a sophomore in high school, and you are asking somebody to go to the prom, that requires some positive self-talk. You want to go into that conversation with a positive attitude. So, you self-coach with self-talk. "You can do this," you say, just like the children's story, *The Little Engine That Could.*

"I wish I had taken more risk." That's the most popular answer to the question "What's one regret you have?" posed to people over eighty years old. What held them back? I don't know, maybe they just didn't have the confidence, the courage. Skydiving, backpacking around Europe, starting a business, joining a club, learning to play the guitar. "I wish I'd given it a try, but I couldn't start." "I might fail." "I know I won't be any good." "It will take too long." "I don't have time. I just don't have the time."

---

[1] "Self-Talk." *Psychology Today.* https://www.psychologytoday.com/us/basics/self-talk.

Stop it! Negative self-talk is *paralyzing*. And it's even worse when you have family and friends who look at life negatively. There's a Scout leader named Jim Sawyer. He's the most positive, uplifting person in the world. He uses words and phrases of sincere praise that come across as almost spiritual. When he talks, I imagine Jesus, Mother Teresa, or the good, Gandhi-type intention.

In our small town during a fundraiser, Jim used to spend considerable time preparing materials, seating charts, and speeches for presenters. He took great care to make sure everyone was comfortable. He would compliment people on even the slightest event—but not that over-the-top, "you look *marvelous, darling*" kind of compliment that is annoying and makes folks uncomfortable.

His compliments were sincere and made people feel good. His compliments were *inspirational*. When you ended a meeting with Jim, you felt better about yourself. Your self-talk became ultra-positive. "I *do* make a good presentation*!*" "I *am* well organized and ready." "My involvement *does* matter to Scouts."

Jim raised more money and got more people involved than ever before. His raised his voice only when he laughed. His laugh was quick, even when the joke was corny. He made you feel good about yourself. He was the Inspiration Master in every room, and it was all done in a quiet, passionate, selfless way.

Inspiration comes from others. Jim inspired us. We would then be motivated to be like Jim and inspire others.

Go do other things. Like, take more risk, before it's too late.

A Great Way to Improve Attitude

If you want to catch a cold, hang out with people who have a cold; if you want to improve your attitude, hang out with people who have great attitudes.

Like a cold, a positive attitude can be contagious.

So, hang around with people who have great attitudes. Why choose people like Debbie Downer and Eeyore, who are energy draining and want to talk about negative things, when you can go with the opposite of that and be able to spend time with people who looking at the glass as half full?

As the late comedian George Carlin said, "If you have a half a glass of water, you have some say half full. Some say half empty. I say you got a glass twice as big as you need."

Now that is a great attitude. How do you get others to adopt a great attitude? Sometimes it is as simple as the first three words out of your mouth, which is what the next chapter is all about.

Eight Steps to Better Empathy

Did you know the Beatitudes build on one another? I didn't, until recently. Kind of like that song, "The Ankle Bone Connected to the Knee Bone." The progress of the Beatitudes depends on one another, sequentially. If you don't believe me, look it up (the Beatitudes are eight blessings recounted by Jesus during his Sermon on the Mount, recorded in the fifth chapter of the Gospel of Matthew).

Likewise, there is a progression with my eight steps to better empathy. I say *better* empathy because I believe we all have at least a small amount of empathy to start. Some have little empathy while others live a life of empathy. There are lots of levels of empathy, and it comes and goes depending on our life experiences.

Here's a hierarchy of empathy that I made up. There are eight components in the hierarchy—just as there are eight Beatitudes—and they also build on each other. It has absolutely no scientific research or evidence around it. Instead, it's just a nice system to help remember what behaviors *drive* empathy. Here we go:

- **Tone:** The tone of our voice helps others to hear our empathy. The rate, pitch, and volume of our statements of empathy helps express feelings. Usually, but not always, we hear implied empathy when somebody *slows down* speech and lowers the pitch and volume. Say, "I am sad to hear that your dog died," and I'll bet you will automatically say it slow and low. The same with excitement at the opposite end of the spectrum. Say "Mom, we won a new car!" You can't help but say it fast, high, and loud. Tone expresses empathy. It's the *how.*
- **Selected Words:** In our "Say This, Not That, Most of the Time" training programs, word selection matters greatly. "I'm sad to hear your dog died." It's personal. *I'M sad.* It's *my* feeling emulating *your* feeling. It's a pretty safe assumption that the dog owner is sad, too. This selection of words is superior, versus, "I was talking to my brother and heard

your dog died," which is insensitive and selfishly pointless. Words matter. It's the *what* in empathy.

- **Features—Advantages—Benefits (FAB):** The best way to describe a benefit is to describe the *feeling* received. "I came by as soon as I heard your dog died; I'm sad." The dog owner can recognize the extra effort and surely appreciates the love. It's a powerful sentence. A special visit, a sense of urgency, and a sincere feeling (sad). Empathy shows *feelings.*

- **Sentence Bookends:** Those little words or phrases capture the emotion and support the *spirit* of what is said or, said wrongly, can deflate the attempted expression of empathy. Here's a bookend done wrong: "Anyway, I heard your dog died recently." Both bookends are insensitive. *Anyway* indicates there is something more important to discuss. *Recently* shows no sensitivity. The dog owner probably remembers the time of death to the minute, not merely recently. Bookends help *define* the level of empathy.

- **Etiquette:** Empathy is supportive and is shown when we elevate our etiquette. Let's stay with the dead dog situation. When offering condolences, etiquette is much appreciated. The lost art of the handwritten note can be found and used here. I've never received a bad handwritten note. Never. Showing empathy occurs when we slow down, do the little things, and are sincere. That's etiquette--when empathy is *proper and professional.*

- **Listening:** Speaking of lost art, how about the lost art of silence? For some people, the opposite of talking is just waiting to talk. World-class empathy includes world-class listening. Commit, focus, ask questions, take notes. With excellent *listening,* you display great empathy.
- **Defusing Stressful Situations:** Sometimes a call for empathy occurs during tense times. Saying the right thing takes practice, awareness, and usually some foot-in-mouth experiences. Let's say the aforementioned dog got hit by a car. When your first question is, "Did you not have her on a leash," it probably is not going to be received very well. Follow it up with, "Are you going to get another dog," and you have added to the stress. Recognize, restate and reassure: the three *R*s approach to reducing stress and help express empathy. Empathy *acknowledges* stress.
- **Writing with Style:** OK, this one may be a stretch, but expressive writing is cherished by the reader. If you spend the time to thoughtfully and sincerely write your feelings, that card will be impossible to throw away. My wife has a love note I wrote thirty years ago. That makes two people happy. Writing can make empathy *timeless*.

So there you go. Right up the empathy ladder for the "how-to-show" guide. Timeless, acknowledge, listen, professional, definitions, feelings, what and how to express empathy.

The Beatitudes and the "backbone connected to the neck bone" song got nothin' on us.

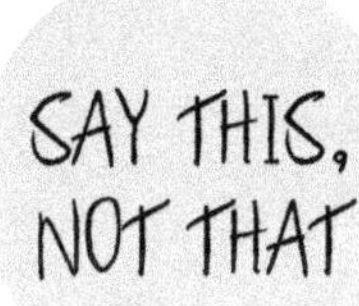

More You, Less Me Attitude

SAY THIS	NOT THAT
Great to see you	I'm here
How's your ankle?	I hurt my knee
Hi, I'm ___________	Do you remember my name?
Gosh, a lot is going on	You look tired

We need to talk.
Oh no.
CartoonStock.com

8

Not What You Say, But How You Say It

Remember: No one in history has ever led a victory charge with a monotone voice. Remember this classic movie line

"Bueller…Bueller…Bueller…"

If you have seen the1986 movie *Ferris Bueller's Day Off*, you always will remember that line. Ferris Bueller's economics teacher, played by Ben Stein, is calling roll and keeps repeating his missing student's name in a monotone. He gets no response.

That scene has become our go-to company's reference in meetings, classes, or conversations when no one is responding. And anyone who has used that reference knows to capture the most critical component—the teacher's completely expressionless voice.

Your natural ability to shift the variety of your voice *tone*—rate, volume, and pitch—is your secret weapon. We must each work to use dynamic vocal variety by adjusting our *tone*.

Varying the dynamics of your voice is a choice you make given the situation or people involved. The situation drives the selection of inflection: library voice or playground voice? You don't use the same voice at a sporting event and a funeral, right? Slow rate for teaching, high volume when coaching a team. High pitch to celebrate, overall confident tone when leading. Also, it's OK to use a tone of uncertainty when problem-solving with a team. "Let's put our heads together to ship the parts before month-end. We don't know how yet, so *help*!"

Dynamic voice variety has a lot to do with the setting you're in and the people involved. We naturally speak differently in different environments. Your choice should match the current situation or surrounding. It should also match your expected outcome for the conversation. If you are telling a child to not run into a busy street, you want the child to feel completely aware and understand the severity of the possible outcome. That's OK in our house.

We spend a lot of time planning what we're going to say. But, then we skimp on planning how we're going to say it. And that can have just as much power. Muhammad Ali's "Float like a butterfly, sting like a bee" interview before his landmark fight with Sonny Liston would have come off *completely different* had he chosen a voice with any less bravado and punch. Sally Field's Oscar acceptance speech featuring the statement "You like me—you really like me" would have come off *completely different* had she ended that sentence as a question rather than a declaration.

The difference in both of those examples is how they used their voice to show confidence.

That's easier said than done, though. Some people approach every scenario with the exact same style of voice. The two strongest culprits? The Valley Girl and the mountain man.

We associate the Valley Girl voice with teenage girls in movies from the 1980s. It's a light, airy, animated, almost cartoonish, whimsical voice first popularized in a 1982 song by the same name by Frank Zappa, featuring a spoken-word monologue by his then-teenaged daughter, Moon Unit. The Valley Girl voice ends on an up-note whether it is a question or a declarative statement. Like, *totally!*

As is often the case with dynamic voice variety, ending on an up-note can be powerful when it's done right. But, use that technique every time, *and it's annoying. As if*!

I hear the Valley Girl voice on the radio a lot. It drives me nuts. It's too casual, perhaps even sloppy. It never accounts for the actual content of the conversation. The kicker is, though, that we oftentimes don't realize we're using it.

At GCS, we've been talking about and coaching to the Valley Girl voice now for fifteen years. It all started with a customer service representative named Lisa James.

One day, Lisa's manager, Dee, delivered feedback to Lisa about how she ends her calls. She said Lisa used "uptalk"—meaning the Valley Girl accent—noting that Lisa ends sentences consistently on that up note. This was news to Lisa. She was completely unaware—even doubtful—that she spoke like that. But because we record all calls, Lisa was able to listen to recordings of herself. And when she did so, she heard exactly what Dee was talking about. Lisa was now able to do something about it. We're able to report that Lisa is no longer a Valley Girl.

Her ability to define the vocal issue meant she could fix it and exude more confidence on every call moving forward. *That is the goal.*

From this process and Lisa's lightbulb moment, GCS created *The FEED Program*. FEED stands for providing quality Feedback to Employees Every Day. Its main purpose is to see that managers are coaching team members on word selection and dynamic voice variety. Every day.

FEED is a crowd pleaser because it does the work on its own. We're in the audio business, and we record all our calls, which means we can give team members the ability to listen to themselves—and their voices. We are 100 percent committed to it so that our team members can hear it, define it, and then improve it, just as Lisa did. Her new level of confidence is the goal.

Another example of dynamic vocal variety is the mountain man. The mountain man ends sentences with a lowered voice. So, he (or she) will begin a sentence in a natural, comfortable range. Then, he (or she) will lower the voice at the end of the sentence.

When the mountain man voice is done right, it's a sign of confidence. The best example of the mountain man voice in modern history is former President Barack Obama. President Obama often utilizes the mountain man voice in a variety of settings that are both casual and professional. The key to using it well is *timing* it well and appropriately. Otherwise, the end of the sentence is inaudible, and the main message might be lost.

PRINCIPLE

When we overuse one method of voice variety, it loses its impact. The key is to use your voice to its greatest impact. Make the choice to slow down and articulate clunkier sentences. Use your playground or stage voice when you need volume. Use uptalk at the end of sentences when there's a *question or genuine excitement.* Utilize the mountain man approach when you need to portray confidence.

Some Ideas on How to Improve Tone

Think of your favorite scene or character from a movie. Perhaps it is a game-changing speech or a powerful scene in which a character delivers a strong monologue. What do you recognize or remember about how he or she uses voice to deliver his or her message?

I suggest starting a notebook (paper or electronic) of hints. Write down the things you want to be able to do when it comes to speaking skills. Then, ask friends or colleagues to write down what they think you do well and what areas for improvement exist for you specifically. *Like, uh, you say* like *and* uh *too much. And you talk too loud sometimes.*

When we look at tone, we approach it from the academic standpoint: tone equals the rate in which you speak, the volume at which you speak, and the pitch of your voice.

Rate of speech is something anyone can easily coach themselves on. The common spoken words-per-minute rate in American English falls in a normal range of 140 to 180 words per minute. Try recording your voice and counting your rate. When you want to really emphasize something, you can slow down. On the other hand, if you know that everybody already knows what you're getting ready to say, you can go ahead and speed up a little bit. Work to get to the point where you've got rate consistency. Then you can still pick your spots for emphasis by consciously choosing different rates.

The encyclopedia or dictionary will define pitch as the relative highness or lowness of a tone as perceived by the ear, which depends on the number of vibrations per second produced by the vocal cords. Pitch is the main acoustic part of intonation. I liken pitch to playing the piano: two keys down, two keys up. The point is never to speak at the same pitch for an extended period. (Ask Dr. Karl Hales if you don't believe me—more about him in chapter 11).

And lastly, let's consider volume. The only thing to remember about volume is that it's beneficial to keep a listener engaged by changing your volume. Sometimes you want to increase the volume or lower the volume to gain attention or for emphasis (counterintuitively, *lowering* your volume is an excellent way to get someone's attention).

Not What You Say, But How You Say It

SAY THIS	NOT THAT
Vary rate, pitch, volume	Monotone
Statements that end on a same note	Valley Girl statements
Questions that end on a higher pitch	Downbeat mountain man questions
140 to 180 words per minute	Constantly slow or fast pace
Varied pitch	Staying on same pitch
Variance in volume	Staying on same volume

"The Lord spake to Moses? You mean voice mail?"

9

Defuse Difficult Drama

Here are seven magic words that can defuse difficult drama:

"What would you like to see happen?"

Recently a friend sent an email to say he uses this question almost once a week. He learned it during a seminar at our company in the early '90s. What a great question. Every word has a purpose and a value:

- **What:** Be specific
- **Would:** If you *could*, what *would* it be
- **You:** What would *you*, not anybody else
- **Like:** Not *love*, not *want*, but instead, what would you *like*—which is a friendly, emotional word
- **To see:** Not *hear*, but *see*, which helps to visualize the answer or solution
- **Happen:** Not *next*, not *here*, but actually take place—this is the starting point, the action, something we can grasp *to actually do*

This question is great for everything from a crying child to a military negotiation. The question is especially helpful in customer service calls with an upset customer.

Once I spent what seemed like an eternity with an upset insurance customer. The call had been escalated to me after an hour of conversations with our agent, her supervisor, and the center manager. It got to me 600 miles away from the Florida center.

The customer had "flipped the anger switch" and couldn't cut it off. No matter what we said, he would start back at the beginning: The "I can't believe I'm paying for this" rant.

Finally, there was a pause long enough to slowly, purposefully, and sincerely ask the question: "Mr. Smith, what would like to see happen?"

Suddenly, he was empowered and required to be part of the solution. "I want an apology, and I want to make sure the agent gets reprimanded."

This is where you have to be careful. Mr. Smith wanted an apology and then wanted to tell us how to coach our associates. You cannot be too quick to agree in these situations, because Mr. Smith wanted to hear more.

Here's where the two-way street of empowerment comes into play. "Mr. Smith, I'm going to write the apology letter myself today and send it to your home. What address should I use?" Here he had a double win: He got the sincere apology, and he got a letter from the president. Believe me, it was worth my effort to make him a hero.

Now, the two-way street part kicks in. "Mr. Smith, you know running a company with 2,000 employees and two million customer interactions a month can be tricky. I will personally work with the center manager to counsel, coach, and train not just this agent, but all agents. You have helped our company."

The point of "What would you like to see happen?" is that *you don't have to give the person the universe if all they want is a star.*

If I had said, "If we give you a thousand dollars, will you be satisfied?" *Of course* he would have said yes. But he never would have thought about asking for money.

Asking this seven-word question gives you a chance to *actually do something.* And that something might be a lot less than you thought you needed to do to defuse the drama.

Defuse Difficult Situations

Defusing stressful situations or difficult situations encapsulates all the previous chapters. The right words, said the right way, with the right empathy, in the right bookends, give the right framework for that difficult situation.

Focus on the three *R*s: repeat, respect, respond. For people to feel they have been truly heard, it's nice for them to hear their own words repeated back.

For example, consider this stressful situation. A person is calling to report an accident and says, "We had a wreck on Highway 51 at the intersection of Jones Street."

When you repeat back, "OK, Highway 51 at the intersection of Jones Street. All right, I know where that is. Sounds like you're in a pickle right now. A real issue. I am here to help."

This is what the caller is thinking: *Oh, you're listening to me. Good! I've got somebody who's connected to me on this line.*

PRINCIPLE

Being able to accurately repeat the issue, be empathetic, and show respect goes a long way. This is true in work, personal relationships, and family situations.

The worst thing you can say is this: "I don't understand why you're so excited," or "You shouldn't feel bad about that," or "Just calm down." That does not put out the drama fire; it pours gasoline on the flames.

As a parent, sometimes you might be called upon to break up two kids fighting. Instead of telling the kids to calm down, trying asking them each the seven-word magic question: *What would you like to see happen?* The act of thinking of the answer to that question has a calming effect.

This works with strangers, too. Once I dialed down the drama in the Atlantis Paradise Island Casino in the Bahamas with a man who was the starting offensive tackle for the Oakland Raiders. He had just been asked (OK, *required*) to leave a craps table for bad behavior. This guy is massive—easily three times my size. I didn't know who he was, and I did not work for the casino. I just saw a frustrated person about ten feet away from the craps tables. I simply went over and talked to him.

"What happened?" He talked about what had happened and his frustration. I said, "What would you like to see happen?" Really, I had no power to help; I was merely another guest. But just talking about it cooled him down.

When you manage a company, you get lots of practice cooling people down. Every thirty minutes in our transit call center in New York, somebody with a disability needs help.

Our internal expression for this? Somebody is in a foxhole (which is a small pit soldiers dig to take refuge from enemy fire). When we say the caller is in a foxhole, we mean they are in a tough spot when they call. A person may be confined to a wheelchair and is on a sidewalk trying to catch a bus. When people in foxholes call, one of the biggest things that can be done to make them feel comfortable is to prove you are listening by telling them where they are.

An upset caller who needs help might say, "I'm at the corner of Fifty-Seventh Street and Eighth Avenue."

Then the customer advocate should say, "I know exactly where you are. I've got it here on the map. Fifty-Seventh Street and Eighth Avenue. Which side of the road are you on? Are you on the side where the theater is or are you on the side where the parking lot is?"

"I'm on the parking lot side," says the caller.

"OK, all right. We've got you. I have somebody eight minutes away. Are you going to be OK?" says the customer advocate.

We instruct our customer advocates to ask callers questions. Get affirmation and confirmation.

Remember, these are not teaching moments. Don't try to educate the person about how they can avoid the problem *next time*. The goal is simply to get them out of the foxhole into safety. That is how to defuse the drama.

Brother Talk That Saved Me

This book is about dumb things we all say. Everybody can learn from their mistakes. I'm really good at it because I have made thousands of them.

When I was a high school junior, my grade point average was below 2.0. Although I was making *C*s and a *D*, I was cool with that, because I was going to play basketball in college. Heck, I barely started on my high school team, but that was my plan—until my brother came to me with his displeasure.

"You are at a crossroads, and it may already be too late," my brother told me.

This was a big brother intervention.

On my report cards every teacher's note said, "Greg is not applying himself," or "Greg is not interested in learning." They were right, and my brother was right. It shook me up.

My senior year was closer to a 4.0 GPA. I jumped into college at UNC-Charlotte with an eye on a business degree (because, like banks, that's where the money is). I even made the Dean's List. But then I transferred to Wake Forest my junior year and experienced one of the worst years of my life emotionally. I was behind in everything. I took too many courses. I lived off campus, isolated from school. I was making straight *C*s again. *No grad school for you, Greg.*

A defining moment was taking an English exam and absolutely choking on the essay part. My writing was so bad that the teacher sent me to remediation. That turned out to be a *very good penalty* for me.

The remedial writing instructor said, "Write about something you love and know about." I chose jazz music. My words, sentences, and paragraphs could have been liner copy for Blue Note Records. The instructor didn't know why I was there. I did, but now I had my groove. Later that year, I got invited to the university president's office. I had written an essay on "The Comedy of Watergate," and he thought it was hilarious and wanted to meet me. It was a proud moment and a long way from my high school low.

But, I was also a long way from grad-school-worthy grades and was paying the dues for not applying myself in earlier years. So, I transferred again—to the greatest small college in the universe, Catawba College in Salisbury, the hometown school that was right in my backyard growing up. I flourished in class and greatly succeeded in extracurriculars such as booking bands, working with the newspaper, being active in marketing club, and—oh, yeah, big-time success playing intramural basketball.

I would have never thrived at Catawba without first making mistakes and rebounding from those mistakes. Call it persistence, competitiveness, or just not knowing any better. Today, when I mess up, I learn from it, shake it off, *fix it,* and don't repeat. Thanks to my brother.

Here is the moral of the story: We all do and say dumb things. Mistakes are a part of life and learning. When it comes to communications mistakes. learn from them, shake it off, *fix it,* and don't repeat.

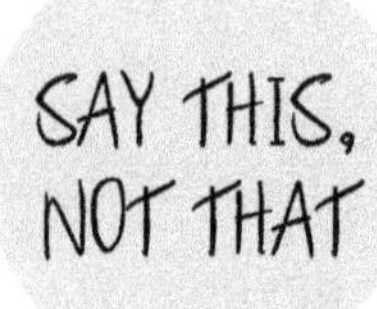

Defuse Difficult Drama

SAY THIS	NOT THAT
Let's keep trying	I/you can't do that
Grow where you are planted	Anything is possible
Take the high road	Give them what they deserve
Stay professional	Burn them to the ground
Be calm and focused	Get jacked up over it

PART III

What Comes Next

" YOUR CALL IS VERY IMPORTANT TO US,
SO PLEASE CONTINUE TO HOLD ."

10

Find Your Practice Buddy

If you want to eliminate the seven dumb mistakes, then practice with a buddy.

When you practice with a buddy, take the phrase "Practice makes perfect" and change it to motivational speaker Dennis Waitley's *"Practice makes permanent."*

Malcolm Gladwell, an author who has been named by *Time* magazine as one of its 100 most influential people, writes about the 10,000-hour principle. His 2005 research shows that to *master* a skill takes 10,000 hours. A concert pianist certainly plays at least 10,000 hours to become great. Pro athletes spend most of their time working on their skills.

Therefore, people in customer service working forty hours a week for five years accumulate 10,000 hours are a likely to be great. Right?

Not so fast. The blended principle should be "*Perfect* practice makes perfect." Otherwise, *bad habits* are simply made permanent.

Here are a couple of examples. My friends in the Appalachian area use the word "went" for "gone" and don't think twice about it. Our clients in New England add an *R* on the end of words that don't have a *R* anywhere close to their standard English pronunciation. (I have no *idear* why.)

To be a student of the game, you first need a teacher. I watched a young golfer practicing what's called a pitch shot. He got a bucket of golf balls and spent about thirty minutes hitting shot after shot with a variety of results. Good shots, poor shots, too long, too short, too high, too low, just right. Everything *but* consistent.

Then, by chance, a golf professional offered to help. After ten minutes of coaching, the young golfer's technique had greatly improved. The scatter graph of his shots became much tighter. (That means most of the shots were the same, and you could throw a blanket over the balls where they landed.)

That young golfer was my son, Clark. Thank goodness, he didn't have to learn from me.

I'm more interested in proficiency than perfection. After watching Gladwell's TED Talk about mastery, I stumbled across one on proficiency by Josh Kaufman, an author and business advisor. Kaufman's message was that with the right type of concentrated effort, you can reach a proficiency level with about anything. His example was learning to play a ukulele. He played quite well and said he gotten to that point with twenty hours of practice. His practice routine was the key: to commit to concentrated, forty-five-minute sessions. Uninterrupted. Every day.

I used this technique to improve my Spanish. Next up for me is to become proficient in playing the drums. My wife is dreading that one.

This is where the buddy system really helps. Practicing in a vacuum with no one around can be difficult. If you have a friend, website, chat room, Skype, coach, or coworker to partner with, learning stays on course and is more enjoyable. You must also have a buddy who can encourage you; if you partner with someone who laughs at your mistakes or gives you grief when you mess up, they can hurt your progress.

Find someone who can not only be your advocate, but also be an accomplice—not just someone who is supportive (an advocate), but someone who gets personally involved in your growth (an accomplice).

" That was a very interesting cell phone conversation. Thanks for sharing it with me. "

11

Write with Style and Avoid Digital Dilemmas

If I could give you one piece of advice on written communications, it would be this: write clearly and concisely.

My two favorite people in writing are J. Peter Kincaid and Rudolf Flesch. They were consultants who worked for the United States Navy, and in 1975, they developed a tool that really help simplify my writing. It can help you, too.

Somewhere deep in the settings of Microsoft Word (this is not an advertisement) Options/Proofing lives the Flesch-Kincaid readability statistics checker. One click and the index developed by these guys will score your writing on a grade level and a 1 to 100 level. Here's their definition:

> *Each readability test bases its rating on the average number of syllables per word and words per sentence. The following sections explain how each test scores your file's readability. Flesch Reading Ease test. This test rates text on a 100-point scale. The higher the score, the easier it is to understand the document.*

My goal is to write at an eighth-grade level. (That means I must up my game since I think like a fifth-grader).

Seriously, the scores really help. We tend to try to show how smart we are in our writing. But in doing so, sometimes our point gets lost.

To illustrate, here's a comparison example:

> *By motivating our participants to collaborate until the competition expired, achieving optimum potential for success was a higher possibility.*

Or

> *The basketball coach said work for a layup before the game ends.*

So, why use a long word when you can use a monosyllabic one? Karl Hales was a theater and public speaking professor at Catawba for decades. He taught us the five rhetorical canons of speech and how to say *police* (it's "puh-LEES," not "POE-lees"). Professor Hales says sentences should be no longer than ten words long. Dang! That last sentence was twelve. Once more: Professor Hales says sentences should be less than ten words. Bam! *Ten words.*

Now, I wouldn't get too wound up about sentence length. Just know our attention span is good for one, maybe two points per sentence. This rule of thumb is helpful when trying to focus attention on one subject at a time.

Brainstorming What to Write

When building an outline for writing an article or chapter, my favorite method is the Galileo Method. It's a method of nonlinear brainstorming.

Here's how: take a blank sheet of paper and draw a small oval in the middle. Write your subject inside the oval. Draw nonconnected lines off the oval and write words representing the subject on those lines. You can probably fit eight to twelve lines. Then, expand each word line with expanded, deeper-dive words or terms.

After completing this exercise, look at the schematic, squint your eyes, and it should look like a deformed octopus holding seaweed. (Remember, I grew up in the '70s.)

With some practice, the Galileo method of brainstorming should provide enough subject matter to give you a paragraph per tentacle. Now that is freaky cool. Right on!

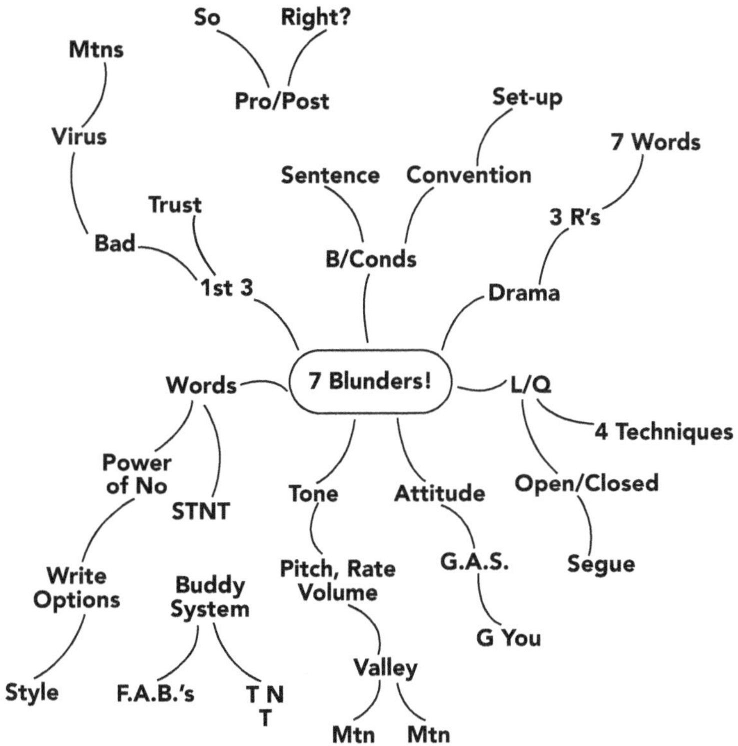

Be Interesting, But Don't Use *Interesting*

"The weather, yesterday, was *wicked.*" That's what an Englishman told me. We were playing golf, and my ball was on a tree root. This predicament is not unusual for my game.

I stared at the ball and said, "This should be an interesting shot."

The Englishman said, "You Americans overuse the word *interesting.* How was the play? Interesting. Anita is coming to dinner. Oh, that should be interesting. That scab on your knee is interesting."

The Englishman gave me a good tip for speaking and writing. Use more descriptive words or terms and have some fun with them. *The weather was wicked.* I'll never forget his description. *If your next shot hits the green, I'll smoke the hen and carve the turkey with dinner on me.* Say what? My likelihood of success was slimmer than Twiggy. (That's might be my best British reference, and if you're younger than I am, you may not get it.)

My writing voice attempts to convey carefree, mindful joy. I copy writing styles that speak this way. A touch of humor, an easy message. A bit of research, a couple principles. I look forward to reading Jason Gay, a sports writer for *The Wall Street Journal.* Seth Godin, Malcolm Gladwell, Tom Peters, and Catawba College's Nelson Murphy write with that same rhythm and cadence.

Remember, facts tell and stories sell. Not only in a business setting, but in teaching, learning, and building relationships. Friends from school bond through shared experiences and memories. Writing these memories with flair and colorful language can symbolize carefree, mindful joy.

PRINCIPLE

Let your keyboard help with tone of voice. The four style tools are boldface, underlining, ALL CAPS, and *italics.* To clearly highlight certain words or terms, these tools provide *COLOR*.

CAPS = LOUD (Typing in ALL CAPS IS SHOUTING)

Underlining = Highlights a change

Bold = Importance and/or a call to action

***Italics* = Higher pitch or emphasis**

The Power of Clear and Concise Writing

Here is an example of the power of clear and concise writing. At my company, our written mission statement ends with, "for this generation and the next." Meaning, we want to be in business for about forty years.

What does it take to have a successful business over a long period of time? Most people would say "luck," and they might be right in some cases. I know we have been lucky to have communicators like Frank Camp.

Once upon a time, Frank saved our company. In 2011, GCS was just starting a rapid decline in business. The Great Recession included the Dodd-Frank Act, which halted big banks from selling group life insurance coverage to customers. That was essentially all GCS did. We started closing centers one at a time. From thirteen to eight during that year and more in 2012. There was negative cash flow and a negative future for banking and insurance marketing, which had been our bread and butter since the late 1980s.

We had one hope: reinvent our company to become an outsourced provider of customer service staffing by winning at least one big program. Enter Frank Camp. Frank was our vice president of customer service. Frank had joined GCS in 2004, and we had also worked together in the '90s. More importantly, Frank was a prolific and very quick writer.

Enter the New York City Transit Authority. The Authority ran the Paratransit Command Center and was bidding out management and staffing. The incumbent was messing up big time; the center was in chaos. Totally toxic. Paratransit means transporting people with disabilities; in that situation, you need organization, not chaos.

David versus Goliath had nothing on our situation. We were small and unproven underdogs in both customer service and the transportation space. While we were David, the incumbent and most everybody quoting the program were large, multinational companies. Goliaths.

In hindsight, the hulking and clumsy, overconfident giants were irritating to the decision-makers.

And we had a secret weapon: Frank.

The Request for Proposal (RFP) response process took eighteen months. Our response was over 1,000 pages long, not including spreadsheets. Frank wrote 99 percent of the response.

Within the eighteen-month RFP period, the bidders were reduced from fifteen companies to five and then narrowed to three for special consideration. We made each cut—mainly because Frank wrote clearly and concisely, and the other suitors didn't.

We were still nervous. I announced to our team that we would practice strategic procrastination and delay closing more centers until the Authority decided. We didn't want to scare off the biggest fish we had ever hooked. It was painful and costly to wait, wait, and wait for a decision.

Then the oral presentation process started. Frank put together the best PowerPoint presentation of his life and followed it up with laser-focused responses to the Authority's follow-up questions. The orals took over four months. The clock kept ticking on our cash burn and underutilized call centers. I shielded Frank from the daily details of customer service and let him focus 100 percent on New York.

The client had to decide. Pick the incumbent and hope they could turn around their toxic center, or pick an unproven but experienced call center operator from North Carolina. We shifted into high gear. We offered a facility in Reading, PA, and showcased our ergonomic workstation designs, workforce management processes, and friendly but firm soft-skills training program. That didn't work. They wanted the next contractor to take over the existing center in NYC. *Hot transfer*. This operation is 24/7, so the hand-off had to happen seamlessly with old out, new in.

On November 6, 2012, we won the contract: a quarter-*billion*-dollar, seven-year behemoth contract with the largest paratransit program in the world. Ninety-nine percent of the credit goes to Frank. We celebrated for a couple days and then went to work.

Frank started putting the training materials and the transition schedule together. We had six departments mobilize to begin the preparation for the April 1 (no fooling) takeover of the 30,000 sq. ft., 400-seat center. We mobilized offsite training space, six trainers, ten interviewers, IT setup, financing, and client services.

Over the next four months, we screened 10,000 applicants (it's New York, where everything is big numbers), interviewed 3,250 (all with paper applications filed by day), and hired 700—but they couldn't start training for more than a month. The training became tricky because we had miscalculated the space requirements and didn't have enough room for our standard training program. Frank had a suggestion: instead of training in two shifts for eight hours, we could train for five hours and three shifts. Sounds simple now, but it took us four days to come to that brilliant solution.

Easter Sunday, April 1, 2013, at midnight, the first GCS employee clocked in at the Paratransit Command and Control Center for New York City. Frank and every vice president and I stayed awake for forty straight hours making sure the transition occurred smoothly. Of course, *it wasn't smooth*, but after a few weeks, we completed the learning curve and have achieved target service levels every month.

The Paratransit Command Center went from a madhouse known for its rudeness and lack of customer service to a five-star darling of the MTA. All because of Frank. Without Frank, I'd be writing about the company's past. Now, we have the present and future, too.

Today, our Transit Authority clients are satisfied with our partnership (as *Seinfeld* fans already know, New York people are either mad or not mad; they're never really *happy*). Tom Chin, our key contact, said he would work an extra two years before retiring, because of our company. All because of our hero, Frank Camp.

12

And in Closing

Let's end with a smart roadmap to avoid saying dumb things.

To recap, pay attention to these seven areas and you will be an excellent communicator:

1. **Choose Your Words Well.** The words you choose paint a picture for the listener. Your words express your attitude and your personality.

2. **Use the Right Tone.** People feel more comfortable when they hear a pleasant, variable vocal tone quality. Voice tone is made up of rate, pitch, and volume.

3. **Bracket with Bookends.** Conversation bookends are the small comments or questions we use before or right after a full statement or request for action. Start and end with power.

4. **Ask Great Questions and Really Listen.** Meaningful questions always stay on subject, keep a conversation moving forward, and ensure the other person feels heard and understood. Become a great listener and make an active choice to listen.

5. **Focus on a You Attitude.** Take the *I* and *me* statements out of your conversations and put in the word *you*. This is not a technique; this is an attitude.

6. **Start with Great First Words.** Conversations, like everything, have first impressions, and they begin with your first three words. Hint: one of the words should be the other person's name.

7. **Defuse Difficult Drama.** Stressful conversations, or drama, can be avoided by mastering word selection, listening, and questioning skills. Stressful situations can be defused when you apply the three *R*s: recognize, restate, and reassure.

Do You Have A Servant's Heart?

Do you know the custodian's name? That's the final exam question for teaching the lesson of treating everyone equally.

When I visit our customer service centers, I always seek out the cleaning people. I want to know if they have enough resources, enough supplies, and enough time to keep the center in tip-top shape.

In our office environment, the common areas are the parking lot, break rooms, and bathrooms. Just as in a restaurant, you know when the high-traffic times occur for each area. You prepare for the rush before and just after those times to make sure these areas show respect for your staff.

We preach that we have an upside-down organization chart. On a day-to-day basis, the most important person in our organization is the person on the front lines. The associate speaking to the customer is the most important person in our organization.

As president, I'm the least important person on a day-to-day basis. However, the president should be one of the most influential people in the *long term*. So, when a president is observing daily activities, here are some of the "servant leadership" activities that show genuine respect for front-line associates:

- **Budget an Extra Five Minutes.** Walking quickly past lots of employees does more harm than good. You may think they appreciate your sense of urgency, but it's the opposite. You're showing them that where you're going is more important than they are. Instead, plan your walk. Add an extra five minutes in front of your 10:00 meeting. Then, use that time to engage with associates. You never know; something serendipitous might happen.
- **Take a Knee.** A cardinal sin in office etiquette is standing over an associate. You know what I mean. An associate is sitting, hands on keyboard, eyes on a screen, and the manager is closely towering over them. Too closely. This posture might be appropriate for a student/teacher situation, but in the workplace, there's a better option. The "take a knee" principle lets you demonstrate genuine interest by being on eye level with the seated associate and lets you see the process from their level. Plus, everyone is watching. By taking a knee, you're acknowledging you're on their team. By

hovering over them, you're just the boss. I want associates to work *with*, not *for* me.

- **Wave like Arnold Palmer.** His nickname in golf was "The King." He changed the sport with his personality as much as his performance. Arnold Palmer was known for his charisma and his connection with fans. When he waved at the crowd, you would think he knew every one of them. He used a full-arm, extended wave. A no-doubt-I'm-waving-at-you wave. That's the way I like to wave at people. It makes them feel good and makes our connection that much more personal and purposeful. When you wave at people, leave no doubt about its meaning. The Palmer full-outstretched wave just feels good.
- **Write a Thank-You Note.** When an army general sends a private home to be with his expecting wife, 10,000 soldiers know about it the next day. During a site visit, I needed a ride back to the hotel. An intern obliged, and I wrote him a thank-you note that evening. Ten years later (yes, ten) he *showed* me the same note, which he kept in his now-General Manager's office. The lost art of the hand-written note is not lost on everyone. And hopefully, it is not lost on anyone reading this principle. Thank-you notes feel good to read. They also feel good to write.
- **Go Get Lunch.** You can learn a lot about people by the way they eat. I like to buy lunch for our associates as often as possible. Notice, I didn't say "order" lunch, I said "go get." Lunch (and it can

be breakfast, snacks, or dinner, too) gives everyone a chance to show their personality, talk about personal stuff, and build camaraderie. Speaking of lost arts, you can also show off your table manners and social graces. If everyone sees that napkins are important to you, they'll appreciate your attention to detail. If you make sure everyone is served before you are, they'll know you practice servant leadership. Getting lunch is not just about the food. Oh, and clean up after everyone, too.

Listen to the Doctor and Take Care of Yourself

I always look for a reason to pass along principles from Dr. Gerald Bell. In his book, *The Achiever*, he outlines the traits for being a good person. Not just a good communicator, but a good person.

One of his chapters talks about the Five Horsemen of Death. It's a morbid name for five categories of managing your life, but it certainly sends the right message. Do them right, and your chances of living longer are better. Do them wrong, and your chances are reduced. The five are diet, exercise, sleep, stress, and safety.

Dr. Bell goes into detail on each one and they all seemed self-explanatory until safety management. That one was eye opening to me. Do you know someone who has fallen off a ladder? Had a skateboard accident? Tripped on a curb while texting?

If you avoid unnecessary risk, you'll live longer. I have now created a phobia of roofs, road biking, and dogs on leashes. Weird, right? My brain says a dog *on* a leash will bite you to protect its owner. I said it was weird.

In addition to being a better communicator, I hope you strive to manage the five horsemen and be safe. Oh, do you know someone willing to clean out the gutters at my house? I'm not getting up there!

APPENDIX A

Summaries

How Not to Lose Friends and Repel People

SAY THIS	NOT THAT
I am great	I am OK
I know exactly what you mean	Yeah, whatever
I'm so sorry that happened	Sorry, that's how it goes
Tell me *your* story	Where are you from?
Listen to this!	Here's a funny story
That's fine	You're fine
We're open until five	We close at five

What to Say and How to Say It: Fixing Seven Common Blunders

SAY THIS	NOT THAT
Thank you for holding	Sorry you had to hold
Tell me your situation	What's your problem?
No wonder you are upset	Take it easy
Has this been helpful?	Guess we're done here
That must have really upset you	Take it easy; just be calm
May I put you on hold?	Hold, please
I'm researching now	Our system is slow today

Beware Your Bookends

SAY THIS	NOT THAT
Mary, thank you for holding	Hello? Are you still there?
May I ask a favor?	Please hold, back in a sec
OK if I look up your account?	Let me see what we have on you
I have three questions, and one comment	Let's talk

Focus on First Few Words

SAY THIS	NOT THAT
I need your help	We need to talk
Share your thought process	Why did you do that?
Help me out	What were you thinking?
I trust you	Better convince me
Help me clarify	I don't believe you
Let's *fix it*	We got big trouble
Let's find the root cause	I'm confused

Choose Your Words Well

SAY THIS	NOT THAT
Sanitation worker	Garbage man
Customer advocates	Call takers
Coverage	Insurance
Children	Kids
Police officers	Cops
You're welcome	No problem
I hear you	Go on

Ask Questions and Master Listening

SAY THIS	NOT THAT
Tell me more	I can top that
Tell me your backstory	How long have you done your job?
What's your story?	Where are you from?
Start from the beginning	When did you meet?
Tell me about him/her	How old is he/she?

More You, Less Me Attitude

SAY THIS	NOT THAT
Great to see you	I'm here
How's your ankle?	I hurt my knee
Hi, I'm ___________	Do you remember my name?
Gosh, a lot is going on	You look tired

Not What You Say, But How You Say It

SAY THIS	NOT THAT
Vary rate, pitch, volume	Monotone
Statements that end on a same note	Valley Girl statements
Questions that end on a higher pitch	Downbeat mountain man questions
140 to 180 words per minute	Constantly slow or fast pace
Varied pitch	Staying on same pitch
Variance in volume	Staying on same volume

Defuse Difficult Drama

SAY THIS	NOT THAT
Let's keep trying	I/you can't do that
Grow where you are planted	Anything is possible
Take the high road	Give them what they deserve
Stay professional	Burn them to the ground
Be calm and focused	Get jacked up over it

APPENDIX B

Acknowledgments

Thanks to Dick Virtue, Chris Virtue, Mike Prillaman, Bart Edge, and all the folks at Southern Alloy and SOMAR. In the 1980s, they believed in me, didn't fire me when they could have, nurtured me, let me join Young Presidents' Organization, and introduced Bell Leadership. And they helped me start a writing discipline that created a library of almost 250,000 words of updates, success stories, lessons learned, and principles.

Thanks to Bryan Overcash, Frank Camp, George Simons, Julie Hlavacek, and all the folks at GCS. In 2001, we started the company with no clients, centers, or employees. For two decades, we continued to surround ourselves with great talent and clients. And the whole time, we collected stories and examples of what to say and not say.

Thanks to all the nonprofit directors, board members, and participants. If you want to learn about yourself, join a nonprofit board. I recommend Catawba College, United Church Homes and Services, NC State Board of Education, Families First, ApSeed and NC Early Childhood Foundation, (Boy) Scouts of America, First United Church of Christ, Novant Health, First Tee, and Rotary Club, to name a lot.

Thanks to my entire family: Missie and our children, Clark and Eleanor; parents, Rev. Ed and Edith Alcorn; and my siblings, Lowell, Bayard, and Janice; and, our eight fantastic nephews and niece. That's right, just one niece.

Thanks to my friends who don't mind telling me when to "turn off the critiques" and when "that's not funny": Miles Busby, John Spencer, Mark and Cliff Ritchie, Marty Meyer, Jim Whitton, David Swaim, Carrie Poole, Tony Leach, Rev. Carol Hallman, Frank Adams III, Victor Wallace, Mona Lisa Wallace, Nelson Murphy, the Jason Walser family, Jake Alexander, Sallie and Derick Close, Patsy Rendleman, Gerry Hurley, Leslie Dent, Mark and Paula Domske, Charles Gaither, Andy Abramson, Bucky Cline, Luke and Diane Fisher, Fred and Alice Stanback, Brien Lewis, Jim Reilly, Ray Oxendine, all the Post/Zimmerman family, and The Trailer Park Forum.

And thanks to Henry DeVries and the wonderful folks at Indie Books International. Their step-by-step approach to putting thoughts, stories, and principles on paper made this book possible. You know what I mean?

APPENDIX C

Further Resources

Global Contact Services: Our staffing and management company specializing in customer service. Our clients benefit from over three decades of hands-on, eyes-on micromanagement. We are an outsourcing contractor for customer-facing and back-office functions. We do it all—outsource, operate, build, and assess all things customer-service centric. www.gcsagents.com

Say This, Not That: Soft-skills training programs featuring principles in the book, plus a lot more. Our online or on-premise modules teach empathy, patience, and can be customized for hot topics. This training combines proven behavioral tools with common sense. The full program name is *Say This, Not That, Most of the Time*. Soft skills are not always absolute dos and don'ts. We explain why.

Hierarchy of Empathy: Maslow's hierarchy provides the pyramid and we replace needs with empathy. Download the illustration and explanations at www.gcsagents.com

ApSeed Early Childhood Education: No telling where ApSeed will be when you read this book. Right now, it's growing like your cousin's three-year-old child you only see twice a year. ApSeed is providing free eReaders to needy children under the age of five. The eReaders are currently producing fantastic results, helping prepare *all* children for kindergarten. www.ApSeed.org

Hierarchy of Reads: We have a fetish for pyramids, I guess. ApSeed only works if a child's basic needs of nutrition and love are covered. Download the hierarchy at www.ApSeed.org.

Bell Leadership Institute: The best resource in the world for leadership development, and not just business leadership. Bell works for family and personal improvement, too. www.BellLeadership.com

APPENDIX D

About the Author

Greg Alcorn is the CEO of Global Contact Services (GCS). GCS, which Alcorn founded in 2001, has served retail, insurance, financial, and government clients for more than fifteen years. It provides clients with outsourced staffing and management for customer interactions.

Greg has lived in Salisbury, North Carolina since he was eight years old and grew up on the Catawba College campus, graduated from Salisbury High School and then graduated with a bachelor's degree from Catawba before earning his MBA from UNC Charlotte.

He and wife, Missie, are the founders of Appleseed, a privately funded pilot program that works to expose at-risk children to books and literacy tools to help them be kindergarten-ready.

Greg was tapped to serve on the Catawba College Board of Trustees in 1999 and has served on a variety of its committees, including finance, enrollment, governance, and audit. He has also served on Catawba's Chiefs Club board, its Green Revolving Fund committee, and a presidential search committee. Catawba honored him with its Distinguished Alumnus Award in 2010, the Church-College Award in 2015, and the Shuford Award in 2016.

He serves on a variety of boards, including the United Church Homes and Services, the North Carolina State Board of Education, Families First, the First UCC Foundation, and Waterworks Visual Arts Center.

He is active with The First Tee of Salisbury, Boy Scouts, and his church, First United Church of Christ in Salisbury. He is a member of the World Presidents' Organization.

Greg and Missie have been married for twenty-five years and are parents of wonderful adult children, Clark and Eleanor.

On a personal note, Greg is a lifelong learner and is ready to learn the drums, much to the dismay of Missie.

APPENDIX E

Index

www.ingramcontent.com/pod-product-compliance
Lightning Source LLC
Chambersburg PA
CBHW031944190326
41519CB00007B/660

* 9 7 8 1 9 4 7 4 8 0 3 2 2 *